THE Ultimate

Chefman

AIR FRYER

COOKBOOK

200 DELICIOUS, CRISPY & EASY-TO-PREPARE

AIR FRYER RECIPES FOR FAST & HEALTHY MEALS

ROBERT ELLINGTON

CONTENTS

INTRODUCTION

Getting to Know Your Chefman Air Fryer

An air fryer is actually a lot like a countertop convection oven. It's a small electric appliance with a heating element and a fan that blows air around in a cooking chamber. However, in an air fryer, the air is swirled very quickly in a circular fashion — so it does a better job of reaching all of the surfaces of the food and creating a crisp crust. Plus, the food itself sits in a perforated basket which increases its contact with the hot moving air. Another thing that makes a big difference? The fact that there's not much space between the walls of the chamber, and the basket intensifies the heat.

The Benefits You'll Chefman Your Gourmia Air Fryer

1. WEIGHT LOSS POTENTIAL

If you're driven to lose weight, you can do so by slowly making changes in your eating and cooking habits. Research shows that cooking your food with an air fryer (versus a deep fryer) can be healthier, thus potentially reducing your caloric intake and contributing to weight loss. Considering that fried food can factor into obesity, weight loss potential is among the most compelling draws of the air fryer. Additionally, the need for significantly less oil helps consumers be mindful of their cholesterol levels. Since air fryers only require a few drops of oil, it's easier to enjoy comfort food faves, like French fries, while keeping minimal saturated fat content.

2. FASTER FOOD PREP

Air fryers are very time-efficient. Foods including chicken, fish, potatoes, and vegetables all cook quickly in an air fryer. This ability is attributed to technology that allows the air fryer to blow hot air evenly within the device.

3. EASIER CLEAN UP

Not only will you exert less effort and spend less time cooking with an air fryer, but you'll also have a much easier time cleaning up. Many of its parts are designed to be wiped off with a damp cloth or washed in the sink with soap. Some air fryers even have parts that are dishwasher-safe. Overall, they're much easier to clean and maintain than larger cooking gadgets.

4. MORE SPACE, LESS STINK

Air fryers also take up less space in the kitchen, which is especially beneficial if you have a smaller space. Another bonus: An air fryer won't leave your house with lingering fried food smells for hours after cooking.

5. GREAT FOR PICKY VEGETABLE EATERS

Are you and your loved ones picky vegetable eaters? Air frying is a great way to crisp up vegetables and make them tastier. Many people enjoy the texture of vegetables such as cauliflower, broccoli, or Brussels sprouts better once they've been air fried. There are also a myriad of online recipes that give options for breading vegetables to cook in the air fryer. Some even incorporate lighter options like rice- or chickpea-based crumbs.

How You Should Start with Your Chefman Air Fryer

1. PREPARATION OF THE FOOD

To prevent the food from sticking to the fryer basket, add bare minimum oil.

Let space between the food to allow the hot air to pass through and cook from all sides. Use an aluminum foil paper as a separator.

If you are using marinated or oily ingredients then pat them dry. This will avoid any splattering or excess smoke. Remove any oil / fat from the bottom of the fryer.

2. PREPARATION OF THE CHEFMAN AIR FRYER

Plug in the fryer and preheat it for about 5 minutes.

Ensure that your air fryer is hot enough.

Place the food items inside and avoid overcrowding. Air must be able to circulate through all the sides of each food item to properly cook it.

If you are cooking pre-made foods, you can change the initial oven temperature by 70 degrees and cut the cooking time in half.

3. COOKING IN THE CHEFMAN AIR FRYER

While cooking small food items like chicken wings or fries, try to shake the fryer around a couple of times. Also try rotating the food items every five minutes to guarantee an all-rounded fry.

If you are cooking high fat food, you will find that it releases fat in the base of the fryer. You would need to remove this fat after cooking.

Better to Care for Your Chefman Air Fryer

1. UNPLUG AND ALLOW TO COOL

After every use, unplug the air fryer from the wall outlet and allow the unit to cool completely before cleaning any component.

Wash Removable Components

Once the unit is cool, remove the crisper plate or tray and basket. These can be hand washed with dish-washing liquid and hot water or placed in the dishwasher. Always check the user guide that came with the air fryer to make sure these components are dishwasher-safe. Most manufacturers recommend hand-washing the baskets to extend their life.

2. DRY THE COMPONENTS

If you are handwashing or stop the dishwasher before the drying cycle, use a lint-free microfiber cloth to dry the crisper plate and basket. Never put damp components back into the base unit.

Wipe Down the Base Unit

Dampen a non-abrasive sponge with warm water and add a drop of dish-washing liquid. With the unit unplugged and with the basket, plates or trays removed, use the sponge to wipe out the entire interior opening. Use a microfiber cloth to thoroughly dry the area.

Rinse out the sponge and use it to wipe down the exterior of the appliance including the control panel.

3. DO A DEEP CLEAN

After several uses, check the heating element for grease splatters or food particles. Use a damp non-abrasive sponge to wipe it clean.

If the air fryer develops a bad odor, there are food splatters somewhere in the interior. In a small bowl, mix one tablespoon of water with two tablespoons of baking soda to make a paste. Dip a dampened sponge in the paste to clean the interior. You may also need to use a small soft-bristled brush like a bottle brush or an old toothbrush dipped in the solution to get into all of the corners.

Rinse with a sponge dipped in clean water and dry thoroughly with a microfiber cloth before reinserting the basket and plates and plugging the unit into a wall outlet.

Vegetarians Recipes

Charred Cauliflower Tacos

Servings: 4
Cooking Time: 10 Minutes

Ingredients:
- 1 head cauliflower, washed and cut into florets
- 2 tablespoons avocado oil
- 2 teaspoons taco seasoning
- 1 medium avocado
- ½ teaspoon garlic powder
- ¼ teaspoon black pepper
- ¼ teaspoon salt
- 2 tablespoons chopped red onion
- 2 teaspoons fresh squeezed lime juice
- ¼ cup chopped cilantro
- Eight 6-inch corn tortillas
- ½ cup cooked corn
- ½ cup shredded purple cabbage

Directions:
1. Preheat the air fryer to 390°F.
2. In a large bowl, toss the cauliflower with the avocado oil and taco seasoning. Set the metal trivet inside the air fryer basket and liberally spray with olive oil.
3. Place the cauliflower onto the trivet and cook for 10 minutes, shaking every 3 minutes to allow for an even char.
4. While the cauliflower is cooking, prepare the avocado sauce. In a medium bowl, mash the avocado; then mix in the garlic powder, pepper, salt, and onion. Stir in the lime juice and cilantro; set aside.
5. Remove the cauliflower from the air fryer basket.

6. Place 1 tablespoon of avocado sauce in the middle of a tortilla, and top with corn, cabbage, and charred cauliflower. Repeat with the remaining tortillas. Serve immediately.

Falafel

Servings: 4
Cooking Time: 10 Minutes

Ingredients:
- 1 cup dried chickpeas
- ½ onion, chopped
- 1 clove garlic
- ¼ cup fresh parsley leaves
- 1 teaspoon salt
- ¼ teaspoon crushed red pepper flakes
- 1 teaspoon ground cumin
- ½ teaspoon ground coriander
- 1 to 2 tablespoons flour
- olive oil
- Tomato Salad
- 2 tomatoes, seeds removed and diced
- ½ cucumber, finely diced
- ¼ red onion, finely diced and rinsed with water
- 1 teaspoon red wine vinegar
- 1 tablespoon olive oil
- salt and freshly ground black pepper
- 2 tablespoons chopped fresh parsley

Directions:
1. Cover the chickpeas with water and let them soak overnight on the counter. Then drain the chickpeas and put them in a food processor, along with the onion, garlic, parsley, spices and 1 tablespoon of flour. Pulse in the food processor until the mixture has broken down into a coarse

paste consistency. The mixture should hold together when you pinch it. Add more flour as needed, until you get this consistency.

2. Scoop portions of the mixture (about 2 tablespoons in size) and shape into balls. Place the balls on a plate and refrigerate for at least 30 minutes. You should have between 12 and 14 balls.

3. Preheat the air fryer to 380°F.

4. Spray the falafel balls with oil and place them in the air fryer. Air-fry for 10 minutes, rolling them over and spraying them with oil again halfway through the cooking time so that they cook and brown evenly.

5. Serve with pita bread, hummus, cucumbers, hot peppers, tomatoes or any other fillings you might like.

Eggplant Parmesan

Servings: 4
Cooking Time: 8 Minutes Per Batch

Ingredients:

- 1 medium eggplant, 6–8 inches long
- salt
- 1 large egg
- 1 tablespoon water
- ⅔ cup panko breadcrumbs
- ⅓ cup grated Parmesan cheese, plus more for serving
- 1 tablespoon Italian seasoning
- ¾ teaspoon oregano
- oil for misting or cooking spray
- 1 24-ounce jar marinara sauce
- 8 ounces spaghetti, cooked
- pepper

Directions:

1. Preheat air fryer to 390°F.

2. Leaving peel intact, cut eggplant into 8 round slices about ¾-inch thick. Salt to taste.

3. Beat egg and water in a shallow dish.

4. In another shallow dish, combine panko, Parmesan, Italian seasoning, and oregano.

5. Dip eggplant slices in egg wash and then crumbs, pressing lightly to coat.

6. Mist slices with oil or cooking spray.

7. Place 4 eggplant slices in air fryer basket and cook for 8 minutes, until brown and crispy.

8. While eggplant is cooking, heat marinara sauce.

9. Repeat step 7 to cook remaining eggplant slices.

10. To serve, place cooked spaghetti on plates and top with marinara and eggplant slices. At the table, pass extra Parmesan cheese and freshly ground black pepper.

Thai Peanut Veggie Burgers

Servings: 6
Cooking Time: 14 Minutes

Ingredients:

- One 15.5-ounce can cannellini beans
- 1 teaspoon minced garlic
- ¼ cup chopped onion
- 1 Thai chili pepper, sliced
- 2 tablespoons natural peanut butter
- ½ teaspoon black pepper
- ½ teaspoon salt
- ⅓ cup all-purpose flour (optional)
- ½ cup cooked quinoa
- 1 large carrot, grated
- 1 cup shredded red cabbage
- ¼ cup peanut dressing
- ¼ cup chopped cilantro
- 6 Hawaiian rolls

- 6 butterleaf lettuce leaves

Directions:
1. Preheat the air fryer to 350°F.
2. To a blender or food processor fitted with a metal blade, add the beans, garlic, onion, chili pepper, peanut butter, pepper, and salt. Pulse for 5 to 10 seconds. Do not over process. The mixture should be coarse, not smooth.
3. Remove from the blender or food processor and spoon into a large bowl. Mix in the cooked quinoa and carrots. At this point, the mixture should begin to hold together to form small patties. If the dough appears to be too sticky (meaning you likely processed a little too long), add the flour to hold the patties together.
4. Using a large spoon, form 8 equal patties out of the batter.
5. Liberally spray a metal trivet with olive oil spray and set in the air fryer basket. Place the patties into the basket, leaving enough space to be able to turn them with a spatula.
6. Cook for 7 minutes, flip, and cook another 7 minutes.
7. Remove from the heat and repeat with additional patties.
8. To serve, place the red cabbage in a bowl and toss with peanut dressing and cilantro. Place the veggie burger on a bun, and top with a slice of lettuce and cabbage slaw.

Cheesy Enchilada Stuffed Baked Potatoes

Servings: 4
Cooking Time: 37 Minutes

Ingredients:
- 2 medium russet potatoes, washed
- One 15-ounce can mild red enchilada sauce
- One 15-ounce can low-sodium black beans, rinsed and drained
- 1 teaspoon taco seasoning
- ½ cup shredded cheddar cheese
- 1 medium avocado, halved
- ½ teaspoon garlic powder
- ¼ teaspoon black pepper
- ¼ teaspoon salt
- 2 teaspoons fresh lime juice
- 2 tablespoon chopped red onion
- ¼ cup chopped cilantro

Directions:
1. Preheat the air fryer to 390°F.
2. Puncture the outer surface of the potatoes with a fork.
3. Set the potatoes inside the air fryer basket and cook for 20 minutes, rotate, and cook another 10 minutes.
4. In a large bowl, mix the enchilada sauce, black beans, and taco seasoning.
5. When the potatoes have finished cooking, carefully remove them from the air fryer basket and let cool for 5 minutes.
6. Using a pair of tongs to hold the potato if it's still too hot to touch, slice the potato in half lengthwise. Use a spoon to scoop out the potato flesh and add it into the bowl with the enchilada sauce. Mash the potatoes with the enchilada sauce mixture, creating a uniform stuffing.
7. Place the potato skins into an air-fryer-safe pan and stuff the halves with the enchilada stuffing. Sprinkle the cheese over the top of each potato.
8. Set the air fryer temperature to 350°F, return the pan to the air fryer basket, and cook for another 5 to 7 minutes to heat the potatoes and melt the cheese.

9. While the potatoes are cooking, take the avocado and scoop out the flesh into a small bowl. Mash it with the back of a fork; then mix in the garlic powder, pepper, salt, lime juice, and onion. Set aside.

10. When the potatoes have finished cooking, remove the pan from the air fryer and place the potato halves on a plate. Top with avocado mash and fresh cilantro. Serve immediately.

Parmesan Portobello Mushroom Caps

Servings: 2
Cooking Time: 14 Minutes

Ingredients:
- ¼ cup flour*
- 1 egg, lightly beaten
- 1 cup seasoned breadcrumbs*
- 2 large portobello mushroom caps, stems and gills removed
- olive oil, in a spray bottle
- ½ cup tomato sauce
- ¾ cup grated mozzarella cheese
- 1 tablespoon grated Parmesan cheese
- 1 tablespoon chopped fresh basil or parsley

Directions:
1. Set up a dredging station with three shallow dishes. Place the flour in the first shallow dish, egg in the second dish and breadcrumbs in the last dish. Dredge the mushrooms in flour, then dip them into the egg and finally press them into the breadcrumbs to coat on all sides. Spray both sides of the coated mushrooms with olive oil.
2. Preheat the air fryer to 400°F.
3. Air-fry the mushrooms at 400°F for 10 minutes, turning them over halfway through the cooking process.

4. Fill the underside of the mushrooms with the tomato sauce and then top the sauce with the mozzarella and Parmesan cheeses. Reset the air fryer temperature to 350°F and air-fry for an additional 4 minutes, until the cheese has melted and is slightly browned.
5. Serve the mushrooms with pasta tossed with tomato sauce and garnish with some chopped fresh basil or parsley.

Tacos

Servings: 24
Cooking Time: 8 Minutes Per Batch

Ingredients:
- 1 24-count package 4-inch corn tortillas
- 1½ cups refried beans (about ¾ of a 15-ounce can)
- 4 ounces sharp Cheddar cheese, grated
- ½ cup salsa
- oil for misting or cooking spray

Directions:
1. Preheat air fryer to 390°F.
2. Wrap refrigerated tortillas in damp paper towels and microwave for 30 to 60 seconds to warm. If necessary, rewarm tortillas as you go to keep them soft enough to fold without breaking.
3. Working with one tortilla at a time, top with 1 tablespoon of beans, 1 tablespoon of grated cheese, and 1 teaspoon of salsa. Fold over and press down very gently on the center. Press edges firmly all around to seal. Spray both sides with oil or cooking spray.
4. Cooking in two batches, place half the tacos in the air fryer basket. To cook 12 at a time, you may need to stand them upright and lean some against the sides of basket. It's okay if they're

crowded as long as you leave a little room for air to circulate around them.

5. Cook for 8 minutes or until golden brown and crispy.

6. Repeat steps 4 and 5 to cook remaining tacos.

Mushroom, Zucchini And Black Bean Burgers

Servings: 4

Cooking Time: 18 Minutes

Ingredients:

- 1 cup diced zucchini, (about ½ medium zucchini)
- 1 tablespoon olive oil
- salt and freshly ground black pepper
- 1 cup chopped brown mushrooms (about 3 ounces)
- 1 small clove garlic
- 1 (15-ounce) can black beans, drained and rinsed
- 1 teaspoon lemon zest
- 1 tablespoon chopped fresh cilantro
- ½ cup plain breadcrumbs
- 1 egg, beaten
- ½ teaspoon salt
- freshly ground black pepper
- whole-wheat pita bread, burger buns or brioche buns
- mayonnaise, tomato, avocado and lettuce, for serving

Directions:

1. Preheat the air fryer to 400°F.

2. Toss the zucchini with the olive oil, season with salt and freshly ground black pepper and air-fry for 6 minutes, shaking the basket once or twice while it cooks.

3. Transfer the zucchini to a food processor with the mushrooms, garlic and black beans and process until still a little chunky but broken down and pasty. Transfer the mixture to a bowl. Add the lemon zest, cilantro, breadcrumbs and egg and mix well. Season again with salt and freshly ground black pepper. Shape the mixture into four burger patties and refrigerate for at least 15 minutes.

4. Preheat the air fryer to 370°F. Transfer two of the veggie burgers to the air fryer basket and air-fry for 12 minutes, flipping the burgers gently halfway through the cooking time. Keep the burgers warm by loosely tenting them with foil while you cook the remaining two burgers. Return the first batch of burgers back into the air fryer with the second batch for the last two minutes of cooking to re-heat.

5. Serve on toasted whole-wheat pita bread, burger buns or brioche buns with some mayonnaise, tomato, avocado and lettuce.

Quinoa Burgers With Feta Cheese And Dill

Servings: 6

Cooking Time: 10 Minutes

Ingredients:

- 1 cup quinoa (red, white or multi-colored)
- 1½ cups water
- 1 teaspoon salt
- freshly ground black pepper
- 1½ cups rolled oats
- 3 eggs, lightly beaten
- ¼ cup minced white onion
- ½ cup crumbled feta cheese
- ¼ cup chopped fresh dill
- salt and freshly ground black pepper

- vegetable or canola oil, in a spray bottle
- whole-wheat hamburger buns (or gluten-free hamburger buns*)
- arugula
- tomato, sliced
- red onion, sliced
- mayonnaise

Directions:

1. Make the quinoa: Rinse the quinoa in cold water in a saucepan, swirling it with your hand until any dry husks rise to the surface. Drain the quinoa as well as you can and then put the saucepan on the stovetop to dry and toast the quinoa. Turn the heat to medium-high and shake the pan regularly until you see the quinoa moving easily and can hear the seeds moving in the pan, indicating that they are dry. Add the water, salt and pepper. Bring the liquid to a boil and then reduce the heat to low or medium-low. You should see just a few bubbles, not a boil. Cover with a lid, leaving it askew and simmer for 20 minutes. Turn the heat off and fluff the quinoa with a fork. If there's any liquid left in the bottom of the pot, place it back on the burner for another 3 minutes or so. Spread the cooked quinoa out on a sheet pan to cool.

2. Combine the room temperature quinoa in a large bowl with the oats, eggs, onion, cheese and dill. Season with salt and pepper and mix well (remember that feta cheese is salty). Shape the mixture into 6 patties with flat sides (so they fit more easily into the air fryer). Add a little water or a few more rolled oats if necessary to get the mixture to be the right consistency to make patties.

3. Preheat the air-fryer to 400°F.

4. Spray both sides of the patties generously with oil and transfer them to the air fryer basket in one layer (you will probably have to cook these burgers in batches, depending on the size of your air fryer). Air-fry each batch at 400°F for 10 minutes, flipping the burgers over halfway through the cooking time.

5. Build your burger on the whole-wheat hamburger buns with arugula, tomato, red onion and mayonnaise.

Roasted Vegetable Thai Green Curry

Servings: 4

Cooking Time: 16 Minutes

Ingredients:

- 1 (13-ounce) can coconut milk
- 3 tablespoons green curry paste
- 1 tablespoon soy sauce*
- 1 tablespoon rice wine vinegar
- 1 teaspoon sugar
- 1 teaspoon minced fresh ginger
- ½ onion, chopped
- 3 carrots, sliced
- 1 red bell pepper, chopped
- olive oil
- 10 stalks of asparagus, cut into 2-inch pieces
- 3 cups broccoli florets
- basmati rice for serving
- fresh cilantro
- crushed red pepper flakes (optional)

Directions:

1. Combine the coconut milk, green curry paste, soy sauce, rice wine vinegar, sugar and ginger in a medium saucepan and bring to a boil on the stovetop. Reduce the heat and simmer for 20 minutes while you cook the vegetables. Set aside.

2.   Preheat the air fryer to 400°F.

3.   Toss the onion, carrots, and red pepper together with a little olive oil and transfer the vegetables to the air fryer basket. Air-fry at 400°F for 10 minutes, shaking the basket a few times during the cooking process. Add the asparagus and broccoli florets and air-fry for an additional 6 minutes, again shaking the basket for even cooking.

4.   When the vegetables are cooked to your liking, toss them with the green curry sauce and serve in bowls over basmati rice. Garnish with fresh chopped cilantro and crushed red pepper flakes.

Falafels

Servings: 12

Cooking Time: 10 Minutes

Ingredients:

- 1 pouch falafel mix
- 2–3 tablespoons plain breadcrumbs
- oil for misting or cooking spray

Directions:

1.   Prepare falafel mix according to package directions.

2.   Preheat air fryer to 390°F.

3.   Place breadcrumbs in shallow dish or on wax paper.

4.   Shape falafel mixture into 12 balls and flatten slightly. Roll in breadcrumbs to coat all sides and mist with oil or cooking spray.

5.   Place falafels in air fryer basket in single layer and cook for 5minutes. Shake basket, and continue cooking for 5minutes, until they brown and are crispy.

Pizza Portobello Mushrooms

Servings: 2

Cooking Time: 18 Minutes

Ingredients:

- 2 portobello mushroom caps, gills removed (see Figure 13-1)
- 1 teaspoon extra-virgin olive oil
- ¼ cup diced onion
- 1 teaspoon minced garlic
- 1 medium zucchini, shredded
- 1 teaspoon dried oregano
- ½ teaspoon black pepper
- ¼ teaspoon salt
- ⅓ cup marinara sauce
- ¼ cup shredded part-skim mozzarella cheese
- ¼ teaspoon red pepper flakes
- 2 tablespoons Parmesan cheese
- 2 tablespoons chopped basil

Directions:

1.   Preheat the air fryer to 370°F.

2.   Lightly spray the mushrooms with an olive oil mist and place into the air fryer to cook for 10 minutes, cap side up.

3.   Add the olive oil to a pan and sauté the onion and garlic together for about 2 to 4 minutes. Stir in the zucchini, oregano, pepper, and salt, and continue to cook. When the zucchini has cooked down (usually about 4 to 6 minutes), add in the marinara sauce. Remove from the heat and stir in the mozzarella cheese.

4.   Remove the mushrooms from the air fryer basket when cooking completes. Reset the temperature to 350°F.

5.   Using a spoon, carefully stuff the mushrooms with the zucchini marinara mixture.

6.   Return the stuffed mushrooms to the air fryer basket and cook for 5 to 8 minutes, or until the cheese is lightly browned. You should be able to

easily insert a fork into the mushrooms when they're cooked.

7. Remove the mushrooms and sprinkle the red pepper flakes, Parmesan cheese, and fresh basil over the top.

8. Serve warm.

Roasted Vegetable Lasagna

Servings: 6
Cooking Time: 55 Minutes

Ingredients:

- 1 zucchini, sliced
- 1 yellow squash, sliced
- 8 ounces mushrooms, sliced
- 1 red bell pepper, cut into 2-inch strips
- 1 tablespoon olive oil
- 2 cups ricotta cheese
- 2 cups grated mozzarella cheese, divided
- 1 egg
- 1 teaspoon salt
- freshly ground black pepper
- ¼ cup shredded carrots
- ½ cup chopped fresh spinach
- 8 lasagna noodles, cooked
- Béchamel Sauce:
- 3 tablespoons butter
- 3 tablespoons flour
- 2½ cups milk
- ½ cup grated Parmesan cheese
- ½ teaspoon salt
- freshly ground black pepper
- pinch of ground nutmeg

Directions:

1. Preheat the air fryer to 400°F.

2. Toss the zucchini, yellow squash, mushrooms and red pepper in a large bowl with the olive oil and season with salt and pepper. Air-fry for 10 minutes, shaking the basket once or twice while the vegetables cook.

3. While the vegetables are cooking, make the béchamel sauce and cheese filling. Melt the butter in a medium saucepan over medium-high heat on the stovetop. Add the flour and whisk, cooking for a couple of minutes. Add the milk and whisk vigorously until smooth. Bring the mixture to a boil and simmer until the sauce thickens. Stir in the Parmesan cheese and season with the salt, pepper and nutmeg. Set the sauce aside.

4. Combine the ricotta cheese, 1¼ cups of the mozzarella cheese, egg, salt and pepper in a large bowl and stir until combined. Fold in the carrots and spinach.

5. When the vegetables have finished cooking, build the lasagna. Use a baking dish that is 6 inches in diameter and 4 inches high. Cover the bottom of the baking dish with a little béchamel sauce. Top with two lasagna noodles, cut to fit the dish and overlapping each other a little. Spoon a third of the ricotta cheese mixture and then a third of the roasted veggies on top of the noodles. Pour ½ cup of béchamel sauce on top and then repeat these layers two more times: noodles – cheese mixture – vegetables – béchamel sauce. Sprinkle the remaining mozzarella cheese over the top. Cover the dish with aluminum foil, tenting it loosely so the aluminum doesn't touch the cheese.

6. Lower the dish into the air fryer basket using an aluminum foil sling (fold a piece of aluminum foil into a strip about 2-inches wide by 24-inches long). Fold the ends of the aluminum foil over the top of the dish before returning the basket to the air fryer. Air-fry for 45 minutes, removing the foil for the last 2 minutes, to slightly brown the cheese on top.

7. Let the lasagna rest for at least 20 minutes to set up a little before slicing into it and serving.

Roasted Vegetable, Brown Rice And Black Bean Burrito

Servings: 2
Cooking Time: 20 Minutes

Ingredients:
- ½ zucchini, sliced ¼-inch thick
- ½ red onion, sliced
- 1 yellow bell pepper, sliced
- 2 teaspoons olive oil
- salt and freshly ground black pepper
- 2 burrito size flour tortillas
- 1 cup grated pepper jack cheese
- ½ cup cooked brown rice
- ½ cup canned black beans, drained and rinsed
- ¼ teaspoon ground cumin
- 1 tablespoon chopped fresh cilantro
- fresh salsa, guacamole and sour cream, for serving

Directions:
1. Preheat the air fryer to 400°F.
2. Toss the vegetables in a bowl with the olive oil, salt and freshly ground black pepper. Air-fry at 400°F for 12 to 15 minutes, shaking the basket a few times during the cooking process. The vegetables are done when they are cooked to your liking.
3. In the meantime, start building the burritos. Lay the tortillas out on the counter. Sprinkle half of the cheese in the center of the tortillas. Combine the rice, beans, cumin and cilantro in a bowl, season to taste with salt and freshly ground black pepper and then divide the mixture between the two tortillas. When the vegetables have finished cooking, transfer them to the two tortillas, placing the vegetables on top of the rice and beans. Sprinkle the remaining cheese on top and then roll the burritos up, tucking in the sides of the tortillas as you roll. Brush or spray the outside of the burritos with olive oil and transfer them to the air fryer.
4. Air-fry at 360°F for 8 minutes, turning them over when there are about 2 minutes left. The burritos will have slightly brown spots, but will still be pliable.
5. Serve with some fresh salsa, guacamole and sour cream.

Curried Potato, Cauliflower And Pea Turnovers

Servings: 4
Cooking Time: 40 Minutes

Ingredients:
- Dough:
- 2 cups all-purpose flour
- ½ teaspoon baking powder
- 1 teaspoon salt
- freshly ground black pepper
- ¼ teaspoon dried thyme
- ¼ cup canola oil
- ½ to ⅔ cup water
- Turnover Filling:
- 1 tablespoon canola or vegetable oil
- 1 onion, finely chopped
- 1 clove garlic, minced
- 1 tablespoon grated fresh ginger
- ½ teaspoon cumin seeds
- ½ teaspoon fennel seeds
- 1 teaspoon curry powder
- 2 russet potatoes, diced
- 2 cups cauliflower florets
- ½ cup frozen peas

- 2 tablespoons chopped fresh cilantro
- salt and freshly ground black pepper
- 2 tablespoons butter, melted
- mango chutney, for serving

Directions:

1. Start by making the dough. Combine the flour, baking powder, salt, pepper and dried thyme in a mixing bowl or the bowl of a stand mixer. Drizzle in the canola oil and pinch it together with your fingers to turn the flour into a crumby mixture. Stir in the water (enough to bring the dough together). Knead the dough for 5 minutes or so until it is smooth. Add a little more water or flour as needed. Let the dough rest while you make the turnover filling.

2. Preheat a large skillet on the stovetop over medium-high heat. Add the oil and sauté the onion until it starts to become tender – about 4 minutes. Add the garlic and ginger and continue to cook for another minute. Add the dried spices and toss everything to coat. Add the potatoes and cauliflower to the skillet and pour in 1½ cups of water. Simmer everything together for 20 to 25 minutes, or until the potatoes are soft and most of the water has evaporated. If the water has evaporated and the vegetables still need more time, just add a little water and continue to simmer until everything is tender. Stir well, crushing the potatoes and cauliflower a little as you do so. Stir in the peas and cilantro, season to taste with salt and freshly ground black pepper and set aside to cool.

3. Divide the dough into 4 balls. Roll the dough balls out into ¼-inch thick circles. Divide the cooled potato filling between the dough circles, placing a mound of the filling on one side of each piece of dough, leaving an empty border around the edge of the dough. Brush the edges of the dough with a little water and fold one edge of circle over the filling to meet the other edge of the circle, creating a half moon. Pinch the edges together with your fingers and then press the edge with the tines of a fork to decorate and seal.

4. Preheat the air fryer to 380°F.

5. Spray or brush the air fryer basket with oil. Brush the turnovers with the melted butter and place 2 turnovers into the air fryer basket. Air-fry for 15 minutes. Flip the turnovers over and air-fry for another 5 minutes. Repeat with the remaining 2 turnovers.

6. These will be very hot when they come out of the air fryer. Let them cool for at least 20 minutes before serving warm with mango chutney.

Spicy Vegetable And Tofu Shake Fry

Servings: 4

Cooking Time: 17 Minutes

Ingredients:

- 4 teaspoons canola oil, divided
- 2 tablespoons rice wine vinegar
- 1 tablespoon sriracha chili sauce
- ¼ cup soy sauce*
- ½ teaspoon toasted sesame oil
- 1 teaspoon minced garlic
- 1 tablespoon minced fresh ginger
- 8 ounces extra firm tofu
- ½ cup vegetable stock or water
- 1 tablespoon honey
- 1 tablespoon cornstarch
- ½ red onion, chopped
- 1 red or yellow bell pepper, chopped
- 1 cup green beans, cut into 2-inch lengths
- 4 ounces mushrooms, sliced

- 2 scallions, sliced
- 2 tablespoons fresh cilantro leaves
- 2 teaspoons toasted sesame seeds

Directions:

1. Combine 1 tablespoon of the oil, vinegar, sriracha sauce, soy sauce, sesame oil, garlic and ginger in a small bowl. Cut the tofu into bite-sized cubes and toss the tofu in with the marinade while you prepare the other vegetables. When you are ready to start cooking, remove the tofu from the marinade and set it aside. Add the water, honey and cornstarch to the marinade and bring to a simmer on the stovetop, just until the sauce thickens. Set the sauce aside.

2. Preheat the air fryer to 400°F.

3. Toss the onion, pepper, green beans and mushrooms in a bowl with a little canola oil and season with salt. Air-fry at 400°F for 11 minutes, shaking the basket and tossing the vegetables every few minutes. When the vegetables are cooked to your preferred doneness, remove them from the air fryer and set aside.

4. Add the tofu to the air fryer basket and air-fry at 400°F for 6 minutes, shaking the basket a few times during the cooking process. Add the vegetables back to the basket and air-fry for another minute. Transfer the vegetables and tofu to a large bowl, add the scallions and cilantro leaves and toss with the sauce. Serve over rice with sesame seeds sprinkled on top.

Veggie Burgers

Servings: 4
Cooking Time: 15 Minutes

Ingredients:

- 2 cans black beans, rinsed and drained
- ½ cup cooked quinoa
- ½ cup shredded raw sweet potato
- ¼ cup diced red onion
- 2 teaspoons ground cumin
- 1 teaspoon coriander powder
- ½ teaspoon salt
- oil for misting or cooking spray
- 8 slices bread
- suggested toppings: lettuce, tomato, red onion, Pepper Jack cheese, guacamole

Directions:

1. In a medium bowl, mash the beans with a fork.

2. Add the quinoa, sweet potato, onion, cumin, coriander, and salt and mix well with the fork.

3. Shape into 4 patties, each ¾-inch thick.

4. Mist both sides with oil or cooking spray and also mist the basket.

5. Cook at 390°F for 15minutes.

6. Follow the recipe for Toast, Plain & Simple.

7. Pop the veggie burgers back in the air fryer for a minute or two to reheat if necessary.

8. Serve on the toast with your favorite burger toppings.

Tandoori Paneer Naan Pizza

Servings: 4
Cooking Time: 10 Minutes

Ingredients:

- 6 tablespoons plain Greek yogurt, divided
- 1¼ teaspoons garam marsala, divided
- ½ teaspoon turmeric, divided
- ¼ teaspoon garlic powder
- ½ teaspoon paprika, divided
- ½ teaspoon black pepper, divided
- 3 ounces paneer, cut into small cubes
- 1 tablespoon extra-virgin olive oil
- 2 teaspoons minced garlic

- 4 cups baby spinach
- 2 tablespoons marinara sauce
- ¼ teaspoon salt
- 2 plain naan breads (approximately 6 inches in diameter)
- ½ cup shredded part-skim mozzarella cheese

Directions:
1. Preheat the air fryer to 350°F.
2. In a small bowl, mix 2 tablespoons of the yogurt, ½ teaspoon of the garam marsala, ¼ teaspoon of the turmeric, the garlic powder, ¼ teaspoon of the paprika, and ¼ teaspoon of the black pepper. Toss the paneer cubes in the mixture and let marinate for at least an hour.
3. Meanwhile, in a pan, heat the olive oil over medium heat. Add in the minced garlic and sauté for 1 minute. Stir in the spinach and begin to cook until it wilts. Add in the remaining 4 tablespoons of yogurt and the marinara sauce. Stir in the remaining ¾ teaspoon of garam masala, the remaining ¼ teaspoon of turmeric, the remaining ¼ teaspoon of paprika, the remaining ¼ teaspoon of black pepper, and the salt. Let simmer a minute or two, and then remove from the heat.
4. Equally divide the spinach mixture amongst the two naan breads. Place 1½ ounces of the marinated paneer on each naan.
5. Liberally spray the air fryer basket with olive oil mist.
6. Use a spatula to pick up one naan and place it in the air fryer basket.
7. Cook for 4 minutes, open the basket and sprinkle ¼ cup of mozzarella cheese on top, and cook another 4 minutes.
8. Remove from the air fryer and repeat with the remaining naan.
9. Serve warm.

Lentil Fritters

Servings: 9
Cooking Time: 12 Minutes

Ingredients:
- 1 cup cooked red lentils
- 1 cup riced cauliflower
- ½ medium zucchini, shredded (about 1 cup)
- ¼ cup finely chopped onion
- ¼ teaspoon salt
- ¼ teaspoon black pepper
- ½ teaspoon garlic powder
- ¼ teaspoon paprika
- 1 large egg
- ⅓ cup quinoa flour

Directions:
1. Preheat the air fryer to 370°F.
2. In a large bowl, mix the lentils, cauliflower, zucchini, onion, salt, pepper, garlic powder, and paprika. Mix in the egg and flour until a thick dough forms.
3. Using a large spoon, form the dough into 9 large fritters.
4. Liberally spray the air fryer basket with olive oil. Place the fritters into the basket, leaving space around each fritter so you can flip them.
5. Cook for 6 minutes, flip, and cook another 6 minutes.
6. Remove from the air fryer and repeat with the remaining fritters. Serve warm with desired sauce and sides.

Egg Rolls

Servings: 4
Cooking Time: 8 Minutes

Ingredients:

- 1 clove garlic, minced
- 1 teaspoon sesame oil
- 1 teaspoon olive oil
- ½ cup chopped celery
- ½ cup grated carrots
- 2 green onions, chopped
- 2 ounces mushrooms, chopped
- 2 cups shredded Napa cabbage
- 1 teaspoon low-sodium soy sauce
- 1 teaspoon cornstarch
- salt
- 1 egg
- 1 tablespoon water
- 4 egg roll wraps
- olive oil for misting or cooking spray

Directions:

1. In a large skillet, sauté garlic in sesame and olive oils over medium heat for 1 minute.

2. Add celery, carrots, onions, and mushrooms to skillet. Cook 1 minute, stirring.

3. Stir in cabbage, cover, and cook for 1 minute or just until cabbage slightly wilts.

4. In a small bowl, mix soy sauce and cornstarch. Stir into vegetables to thicken. Remove from heat. Salt to taste if needed.

5. Beat together egg and water in a small bowl.

6. Divide filling into 4 portions and roll up in egg roll wraps. Brush all over with egg wash to seal.

7. Mist egg rolls very lightly with olive oil or cooking spray and place in air fryer basket.

8. Cook at 390°F for 4minutes. Turn over and cook 4 more minutes, until golden brown and crispy.

Vegetable Hand Pies

Servings: 8
Cooking Time: 10 Minutes Per Batch

Ingredients:

- ¾ cup vegetable broth
- 8 ounces potatoes
- ¾ cup frozen chopped broccoli, thawed
- ¼ cup chopped mushrooms
- 1 tablespoon cornstarch
- 1 tablespoon milk
- 1 can organic flaky biscuits (8 large biscuits)
- oil for misting or cooking spray

Directions:

1. Place broth in medium saucepan over low heat.

2. While broth is heating, grate raw potato into a bowl of water to prevent browning. You will need ¾ cup grated potato.

3. Roughly chop the broccoli.

4. Drain potatoes and put them in the broth along with the broccoli and mushrooms. Cook on low for 5 minutes.

5. Dissolve cornstarch in milk, then stir the mixture into the broth. Cook about a minute, until mixture thickens a little. Remove from heat and cool slightly.

6. Separate each biscuit into 2 rounds. Divide vegetable mixture evenly over half the biscuit rounds, mounding filling in the center of each.

7. Top the four rounds with filling, then the other four rounds and crimp the edges together with a fork.

8. Spray both sides with oil or cooking spray and place 4 pies in a single layer in the air fryer basket.
9. Cook at 330°F for approximately 10 minutes.
10. Repeat with the remaining biscuits. The second batch may cook more quickly because the fryer will be hot.

Arancini With Marinara

Servings: 6
Cooking Time: 15 Minutes

Ingredients:
- 2 cups cooked rice
- 1 cup grated Parmesan cheese
- 1 egg, whisked
- ¼ teaspoon dried thyme
- ½ teaspoon dried oregano
- ½ teaspoon dried basil
- ½ teaspoon dried parsley
- 1 teaspoon salt
- ¼ teaspoon paprika
- 1 cup breadcrumbs
- 4 ounces mozzarella, cut into 24 cubes
- 2 cups marinara sauce

Directions:
1. In a large bowl, mix together the rice, Parmesan cheese, and egg.
2. In another bowl, mix together the thyme, oregano, basil, parsley, salt, paprika, and breadcrumbs.
3. Form 24 rice balls with the rice mixture. Use your thumb to make an indentation in the center and stuff 1 cube of mozzarella in the center of the rice; close the ball around the cheese.
4. Roll the rice balls in the seasoned breadcrumbs until all are coated.
5. Preheat the air fryer to 400°F.

6. Place the rice balls in the air fryer basket and coat with cooking spray. Cook for 8 minutes, shake the basket, and cook another 7 minutes.
7. Heat the marinara sauce in a saucepan until warm. Serve sauce as a dip for arancini.

Corn And Pepper Jack Chile Rellenos With Roasted Tomato Sauce

Servings: 3
Cooking Time: 30 Minutes

Ingredients:
- 3 Poblano peppers
- 1 cup all-purpose flour*
- salt and freshly ground black pepper
- 2 eggs, lightly beaten
- 1 cup plain breadcrumbs*
- olive oil, in a spray bottle
- Sauce
- 2 cups cherry tomatoes
- 1 Jalapeño pepper, halved and seeded
- 1 clove garlic
- ¼ red onion, broken into large pieces
- 1 tablespoon olive oil
- salt, to taste
- 2 tablespoons chopped fresh cilantro
- Filling
- olive oil
- ¼ red onion, finely chopped
- 1 teaspoon minced garlic
- 1 cup corn kernels, fresh or frozen
- 2 cups grated pepper jack cheese

Directions:
1. Start by roasting the peppers. Preheat the air fryer to 400°F. Place the peppers into the air fryer basket and air-fry at 400°F for 10 minutes,

turning them over halfway through the cooking time. Remove the peppers from the basket and cover loosely with foil.

2. While the peppers are cooling, make the roasted tomato sauce. Place all sauce Ingredients except for the cilantro into the air fryer basket and air-fry at 400°F for 10 minutes, shaking the basket once or twice. When the sauce Ingredients have finished air-frying, transfer everything to a blender or food processor and blend or process to a smooth sauce, adding a little warm water to get the desired consistency. Season to taste with salt, add the cilantro and set aside.

3. While the sauce Ingredients are cooking in the air fryer, make the filling. Heat a skillet on the stovetop over medium heat. Add the olive oil and sauté the red onion and garlic for 4 to 5 minutes. Transfer the onion and garlic to a bowl, stir in the corn and cheese, and set aside.

4. Set up a dredging station with three shallow dishes. Place the flour, seasoned with salt and pepper, in the first shallow dish. Place the eggs in the second dish, and fill the third shallow dish with the breadcrumbs. When the peppers have cooled, carefully slice into one side of the pepper to create an opening. Pull the seeds out of the peppers and peel away the skins, trying not to tear the pepper. Fill each pepper with some of the corn and cheese filling and close the pepper up again by folding one side of the opening over the other. Carefully roll each pepper in the seasoned flour, then into the egg and finally into the breadcrumbs to coat on all sides, trying not to let the pepper fall open. Spray the peppers on all sides with a little olive oil.

5. Air-fry two peppers at a time at 350°F for 6 minutes. Turn the peppers over and air-fry for another 4 minutes. Serve the peppers warm on a bed of the roasted tomato sauce.

Poultry Recipes

Chicken Flautas

Servings: 6
Cooking Time: 8 Minutes

Ingredients:

- 6 tablespoons whipped cream cheese
- 1 cup shredded cooked chicken
- 6 tablespoons mild pico de gallo salsa
- ⅓ cup shredded Mexican cheese
- ½ teaspoon taco seasoning
- Six 8-inch flour tortillas
- 2 cups shredded lettuce
- ½ cup guacamole

Directions:

1. Preheat the air fryer to 370°F.
2. In a large bowl, mix the cream cheese, chicken, salsa, shredded cheese, and taco seasoning until well combined.
3. Lay the tortillas on a flat surface. Divide the cheese-and-chicken mixture into 6 equal portions; then place the mixture in the center of the tortillas, spreading evenly, leaving about 1 inch from the edge of the tortilla.
4. Spray the air fryer basket with olive oil spray. Roll up the flautas and place them edge side down into the basket. Lightly mist the top of the flautas with olive oil spray.
5. Repeat until the air fryer basket is full. You may need to cook these in batches, depending on the size of your air fryer.
6. Cook for 7 minutes, or until the outer edges are browned.
7. Remove from the air fryer basket and serve warm over a bed of shredded lettuce with guacamole on top.

Tortilla Crusted Chicken Breast

Servings: 2
Cooking Time: 12 Minutes

Ingredients:

- ⅓ cup flour
- 1 teaspoon salt
- 1½ teaspoons chili powder
- 1 teaspoon ground cumin
- freshly ground black pepper
- 1 egg, beaten
- ¾ cup coarsely crushed yellow corn tortilla chips
- 2 (3- to 4-ounce) boneless chicken breasts
- vegetable oil
- ½ cup salsa
- ½ cup crumbled queso fresco
- fresh cilantro leaves
- sour cream or guacamole (optional)

Directions:

1. Set up a dredging station with three shallow dishes. Combine the flour, salt, chili powder, cumin and black pepper in the first shallow dish. Beat the egg in the second shallow dish. Place the crushed tortilla chips in the third shallow dish.
2. Dredge the chicken in the spiced flour, covering all sides of the breast. Then dip the chicken into the egg, coating the chicken completely. Finally, place the chicken into the tortilla chips and press the chips onto the chicken to make sure they adhere to all sides of the breast. Spray the coated chicken breasts on both sides with vegetable oil.
3. Preheat the air fryer to 380°F.

4. Air-fry the chicken for 6 minutes. Then turn the chicken breasts over and air-fry for another 6 minutes. (Increase the cooking time if you are using chicken breasts larger than 3 to 4 ounces.)

5. When the chicken has finished cooking, serve each breast with a little salsa, the crumbled queso fresco and cilantro as the finishing touch. Serve some sour cream and/or guacamole at the table, if desired.

Simple Buttermilk Fried Chicken

Servings: 4

Cooking Time: 27 Minutes

Ingredients:

- 1 (4-pound) chicken, cut into 8 pieces
- 2 cups buttermilk
- hot sauce (optional)
- 1½ cups flour*
- 2 teaspoons paprika
- 1 teaspoon salt
- freshly ground black pepper
- 2 eggs, lightly beaten
- vegetable oil, in a spray bottle

Directions:

1. Cut the chicken into 8 pieces and submerge them in the buttermilk and hot sauce, if using. A zipper-sealable plastic bag works well for this. Let the chicken soak in the buttermilk for at least one hour or even overnight in the refrigerator.

2. Set up a dredging station. Mix the flour, paprika, salt and black pepper in a clean zipper-sealable plastic bag. Whisk the eggs and place them in a shallow dish. Remove four pieces of chicken from the buttermilk and transfer them to the bag with the flour. Shake them around to coat on all sides. Remove the chicken from the flour, shaking off any excess flour, and dip them into the beaten egg. Return the chicken to the bag of seasoned flour and shake again. Set the coated chicken aside and repeat with the remaining four pieces of chicken.

3. Preheat the air fryer to 370°F.

4. Spray the chicken on all sides with the vegetable oil and then transfer one batch to the air fryer basket. Air-fry the chicken at 370°F for 20 minutes, flipping the pieces over halfway through the cooking process, taking care not to knock off the breading. Transfer the chicken to a plate, but do not cover. Repeat with the second batch of chicken.

5. Lower the temperature on the air fryer to 340°F. Flip the chicken back over and place the first batch of chicken on top of the second batch already in the basket. Air-fry for another 7 minutes and serve warm.

Chicken Souvlaki Gyros

Servings: 4

Cooking Time: 18 Minutes

Ingredients:

- ¼ cup extra-virgin olive oil
- 1 clove garlic, crushed
- 1 tablespoon Italian seasoning
- ½ teaspoon paprika
- ½ lemon, sliced
- ¼ teaspoon salt
- 1 pound boneless, skinless chicken breasts
- 4 whole-grain pita breads
- 1 cup shredded lettuce
- ½ cup chopped tomatoes
- ¼ cup chopped red onion
- ¼ cup cucumber yogurt sauce

Directions:

1. In a large resealable plastic bag, combine the olive oil, garlic, Italian seasoning, paprika, lemon, and salt. Add the chicken to the bag and secure shut. Vigorously shake until all the ingredients are combined. Set in the fridge for 2 hours to marinate.

2. When ready to cook, preheat the air fryer to 360°F.

3. Liberally spray the air fryer basket with olive oil mist. Remove the chicken from the bag and discard the leftover marinade. Place the chicken into the air fryer basket, allowing enough room between the chicken breasts to flip.

4. Cook for 10 minutes, flip, and cook another 8 minutes.

5. Remove the chicken from the air fryer basket when it has cooked (or the internal temperature of the chicken reaches 165°F). Let rest 5 minutes. Then thinly slice the chicken into strips.

6. Assemble the gyros by placing the pita bread on a flat surface and topping with chicken, lettuce, tomatoes, onion, and a drizzle of yogurt sauce.

7. Serve warm.

Peachy Chicken Chunks With Cherries

Servings: 4

Cooking Time: 16 Minutes

Ingredients:

- ⅓ cup peach preserves
- 1 teaspoon ground rosemary
- ½ teaspoon black pepper
- ½ teaspoon salt
- ½ teaspoon marjoram
- 1 teaspoon light olive oil
- 1 pound boneless chicken breasts, cut in 1½-inch chunks
- oil for misting or cooking spray
- 10-ounce package frozen unsweetened dark cherries, thawed and drained

Directions:

1. In a medium bowl, mix together peach preserves, rosemary, pepper, salt, marjoram, and olive oil.

2. Stir in chicken chunks and toss to coat well with the preserve mixture.

3. Spray air fryer basket with oil or cooking spray and lay chicken chunks in basket.

4. Cook at 390°F for 7minutes. Stir. Cook for 8 more minutes or until chicken juices run clear.

5. When chicken has cooked through, scatter the cherries over and cook for additional minute to heat cherries.

Poblano Bake

Servings: 4

Cooking Time: 11 Minutes Per Batch

Ingredients:

- 2 large poblano peppers (approx. 5½ inches long excluding stem)
- ¾ pound ground turkey, raw
- ¾ cup cooked brown rice
- 1 teaspoon chile powder
- ½ teaspoon ground cumin
- ½ teaspoon garlic powder
- 4 ounces sharp Cheddar cheese, grated
- 1 8-ounce jar salsa, warmed

Directions:

1. Slice each pepper in half lengthwise so that you have four wide, flat pepper halves.

2. Remove seeds and membrane and discard. Rinse inside and out.

3. In a large bowl, combine turkey, rice, chile powder, cumin, and garlic powder. Mix well.

4. Divide turkey filling into 4 portions and stuff one into each of the 4 pepper halves. Press lightly to pack down.

5. Place 2 pepper halves in air fryer basket and cook at 390°F for 10minutes or until turkey is well done.

6. Top each pepper half with ¼ of the grated cheese. Cook 1 more minute or just until cheese melts.

7. Repeat steps 5 and 6 to cook remaining pepper halves.

8. To serve, place each pepper half on a plate and top with ¼ cup warm salsa.

Chicken Fried Steak With Gravy

Servings: 4

Cooking Time: 10 Minutes Per Batch

Ingredients:

- ½ cup flour
- 2 teaspoons salt, divided
- freshly ground black pepper
- ¼ teaspoon garlic powder
- 1 cup buttermilk
- 1 cup fine breadcrumbs
- 4 tenderized top round steaks (about 6 to 8 ounces each; ½-inch thick)
- vegetable or canola oil
- For the Gravy:
- 2 tablespoons butter or bacon drippings
- ¼ onion, minced (about ¼ cup)
- 1 clove garlic, smashed
- ¼ teaspoon dried thyme
- 3 tablespoons flour
- 1 cup milk
- salt and lots of freshly ground black pepper
- a few dashes of Worcestershire sauce

Directions:

1. Set up a dredging station. Combine the flour, 1 teaspoon of salt, black pepper and garlic powder in a shallow bowl. Pour the buttermilk into a second shallow bowl. Finally, put the breadcrumbs and 1 teaspoon of salt in a third shallow bowl.

2. Dip the tenderized steaks into the flour, then the buttermilk, and then the breadcrumb mixture, pressing the crumbs onto the steak. Place them on a baking sheet and spray both sides generously with vegetable or canola oil.

3. Preheat the air fryer to 400°F.

4. Transfer the steaks to the air fryer basket, two at a time, and air-fry for 10 minutes, flipping the steaks over halfway through the cooking time. This will cook your steaks to medium. If you want the steaks cooked a little more or less, add or subtract a minute or two. Hold the first batch of steaks warm in a 170°F oven while you cook the second batch.

5. While the steaks are cooking, make the gravy. Melt the butter in a small saucepan over medium heat on the stovetop. Add the onion, garlic and thyme and cook for five minutes, until the onion is soft and just starting to brown. Stir in the flour and cook for another five minutes, stirring regularly, until the mixture starts to brown. Whisk in the milk and bring the mixture to a boil to thicken. Season to taste with salt, lots of freshly ground black pepper and a few dashes of Worcestershire sauce.

6. Plate the chicken fried steaks with mashed potatoes and vegetables and serve the gravy at the table to pour over the top.

Chicken Cutlets With Broccoli Rabe And Roasted Peppers

Servings: 2

Cooking Time: 10 Minutes

Ingredients:

- ½ bunch broccoli rabe
- olive oil, in a spray bottle
- salt and freshly ground black pepper
- ⅔ cup roasted red pepper strips
- 2 (4-ounce) boneless, skinless chicken breasts
- 2 tablespoons all-purpose flour*
- 1 egg, beaten
- ⅓ cup seasoned breadcrumbs*
- 2 slices aged provolone cheese

Directions:

1. Bring a medium saucepot of salted water to a boil on the stovetop. Blanch the broccoli rabe for 3 minutes in the boiling water and then drain. When it has cooled a little, squeeze out as much water as possible, drizzle a little olive oil on top, season with salt and black pepper and set aside. Dry the roasted red peppers with a clean kitchen towel and set them aside as well.

2. Place each chicken breast between 2 pieces of plastic wrap. Use a meat pounder to flatten the chicken breasts to about ½-inch thick. Season the chicken on both sides with salt and pepper.

3. Preheat the air fryer to 400°F.

4. Set up a dredging station with three shallow dishes. Place the flour in one dish, the egg in a second dish and the breadcrumbs in a third dish. Coat the chicken on all sides with the flour. Shake off any excess flour and dip the chicken into the egg. Let the excess egg drip off and coat both sides of the chicken in the breadcrumbs.

Spray the chicken with olive oil on both sides and transfer to the air fryer basket.

5. Air-fry the chicken at 400°F for 5 minutes. Turn the chicken over and air-fry for another minute. Then, top the chicken breast with the broccoli rabe and roasted peppers. Place a slice of the provolone cheese on top and secure it with a toothpick or two.

6. Air-fry at 360° for 3 to 4 minutes to melt the cheese and warm everything together.

Cornish Hens With Honey-lime Glaze

Servings: 2

Cooking Time: 30 Minutes

Ingredients:

- 1 Cornish game hen (1½–2 pounds)
- 1 tablespoon honey
- 1 tablespoon lime juice
- 1 teaspoon poultry seasoning
- salt and pepper
- cooking spray

Directions:

1. To split the hen into halves, cut through breast bone and down one side of the backbone.

2. Mix the honey, lime juice, and poultry seasoning together and brush or rub onto all sides of the hen. Season to taste with salt and pepper.

3. Spray air fryer basket with cooking spray and place hen halves in the basket, skin-side down.

4. Cook at 330°F for 30 minutes. Hen will be done when juices run clear when pierced at leg joint with a fork. Let hen rest for 5 to 10minutes before cutting.

Spicy Black Bean Turkey Burgers With Cumin-avocado Spread

Servings: 2
Cooking Time: 20 Minutes

Ingredients:

- 1 cup canned black beans, drained and rinsed
- ¾ pound lean ground turkey
- 2 tablespoons minced red onion
- 1 Jalapeño pepper, seeded and minced
- 2 tablespoons plain breadcrumbs
- ½ teaspoon chili powder
- ¼ teaspoon cayenne pepper
- salt, to taste
- olive or vegetable oil
- 2 slices pepper jack cheese
- toasted burger rolls, sliced tomatoes, lettuce leaves
- Cumin-Avocado Spread:
- 1 ripe avocado
- juice of 1 lime
- 1 teaspoon ground cumin
- ½ teaspoon salt
- 1 tablespoon chopped fresh cilantro
- freshly ground black pepper

Directions:

1. Place the black beans in a large bowl and smash them slightly with the back of a fork. Add the ground turkey, red onion, Jalapeño pepper, breadcrumbs, chili powder and cayenne pepper. Season with salt. Mix with your hands to combine all the ingredients and then shape them into 2 patties. Brush both sides of the burger patties with a little olive or vegetable oil.

2. Preheat the air fryer to 380°F.

3. Transfer the burgers to the air fryer basket and air-fry for 20 minutes, flipping them over halfway through the cooking process. Top the burgers with the pepper jack cheese (securing the slices to the burgers with a toothpick) for the last 2 minutes of the cooking process.

4. While the burgers are cooking, make the cumin avocado spread. Place the avocado, lime juice, cumin and salt in food processor and process until smooth. (For a chunkier spread, you can mash this by hand in a bowl.) Stir in the cilantro and season with freshly ground black pepper. Chill the spread until you are ready to serve.

5. When the burgers have finished cooking, remove them from the air fryer and let them rest on a plate, covered gently with aluminum foil. Brush a little olive oil on the insides of the burger rolls. Place the rolls, cut side up, into the air fryer basket and air-fry at 400°F for 1 minute to toast and warm them.

6. Spread the cumin-avocado spread on the rolls and build your burgers with lettuce and sliced tomatoes and any other ingredient you like. Serve warm with a side of sweet potato fries.

Pickle Brined Fried Chicken

Servings: 4
Cooking Time: 47 Minutes

Ingredients:

- 4 bone-in, skin-on chicken legs, cut into drumsticks and thighs (about 3½ pounds)
- pickle juice from a 24-ounce jar of kosher dill pickles
- ½ cup flour
- salt and freshly ground black pepper
- 2 eggs
- 1 cup fine breadcrumbs
- 1 teaspoon salt

- 1 teaspoon freshly ground black pepper
- ½ teaspoon ground paprika
- ⅛ teaspoon ground cayenne pepper
- vegetable or canola oil in a spray bottle

Directions:

1. Place the chicken in a shallow dish and pour the pickle juice over the top. Cover and transfer the chicken to the refrigerator to brine in the pickle juice for 3 to 8 hours.

2. When you are ready to cook, remove the chicken from the refrigerator to let it come to room temperature while you set up a dredging station. Place the flour in a shallow dish and season well with salt and freshly ground black pepper. Whisk the eggs in a second shallow dish. In a third shallow dish, combine the breadcrumbs, salt, pepper, paprika and cayenne pepper.

3. Preheat the air fryer to 370°F.

4. Remove the chicken from the pickle brine and gently dry it with a clean kitchen towel. Dredge each piece of chicken in the flour, then dip it into the egg mixture, and finally press it into the breadcrumb mixture to coat all sides of the chicken. Place the breaded chicken on a plate or baking sheet and spray each piece all over with vegetable oil.

5. Air-fry the chicken in two batches. Place two chicken thighs and two drumsticks into the air fryer basket. Air-fry for 10 minutes. Then, gently turn the chicken pieces over and air-fry for another 10 minutes. Remove the chicken pieces and let them rest on plate – do not cover. Repeat with the second batch of chicken, air-frying for 20 minutes, turning the chicken over halfway through.

6. Lower the temperature of the air fryer to 340°F. Place the first batch of chicken on top of the second batch already in the basket and air-fry for an additional 7 minutes. Serve warm and enjoy.

Spinach And Feta Stuffed Chicken Breasts

Servings: 4
Cooking Time: 27 Minutes

Ingredients:

- 1 (10-ounce) package frozen spinach, thawed and drained well
- 1 cup feta cheese, crumbled
- ½ teaspoon freshly ground black pepper
- 4 boneless chicken breasts
- salt and freshly ground black pepper
- 1 tablespoon olive oil

Directions:

1. Prepare the filling. Squeeze out as much liquid as possible from the thawed spinach. Rough chop the spinach and transfer it to a mixing bowl with the feta cheese and the freshly ground black pepper.

2. Prepare the chicken breast. Place the chicken breast on a cutting board and press down on the chicken breast with one hand to keep it stabilized. Make an incision about 1-inch long in the fattest side of the breast. Move the knife up and down inside the chicken breast, without poking through either the top or the bottom, or the other side of the breast. The inside pocket should be about 3-inches long, but the opening should only be about 1-inch wide. If this is too difficult, you can make the incision longer, but you will have to be more careful when cooking the chicken breast since this will expose more of the stuffing.

3. Once you have prepared the chicken breasts, use your fingers to stuff the filling into each

pocket, spreading the mixture down as far as you can.

4. Preheat the air fryer to 380°F.

5. Lightly brush or spray the air fryer basket and the chicken breasts with olive oil. Transfer two of the stuffed chicken breasts to the air fryer. Air-fry for 12 minutes, turning the chicken breasts over halfway through the cooking time. Remove the chicken to a resting plate and air-fry the second two breasts for 12 minutes. Return the first batch of chicken to the air fryer with the second batch and air-fry for 3 more minutes. When the chicken is cooked, an instant read thermometer should register 165°F in the thickest part of the chicken, as well as in the stuffing.

6. Remove the chicken breasts and let them rest on a cutting board for 2 to 3 minutes. Slice the chicken on the bias and serve with the slices fanned out.

Philly Chicken Cheesesteak Stromboli

Servings: 2

Cooking Time: 28 Minutes

Ingredients:

- ½ onion, sliced
- 1 teaspoon vegetable oil
- 2 boneless, skinless chicken breasts, partially frozen and sliced very thin on the bias (about 1 pound)
- 1 tablespoon Worcestershire sauce
- salt and freshly ground black pepper
- ½ recipe of Blue Jean Chef pizza dough (see page 229), or 14 ounces of store-bought pizza dough
- 1½ cups grated Cheddar cheese

- ½ cup Cheese Whiz® (or other jarred cheese sauce), warmed gently in the microwave
- tomato ketchup for serving

Directions:

1. Preheat the air fryer to 400°F.

2. Toss the sliced onion with oil and air-fry for 8 minutes, stirring halfway through the cooking time. Add the sliced chicken and Worcestershire sauce to the air fryer basket, and toss to evenly distribute the ingredients. Season the mixture with salt and freshly ground black pepper and air-fry for 8 minutes, stirring a couple of times during the cooking process. Remove the chicken and onion from the air fryer and let the mixture cool a little.

3. On a lightly floured surface, roll or press the pizza dough out into a 13-inch by 11-inch rectangle, with the long side closest to you. Sprinkle half of the Cheddar cheese over the dough leaving an empty 1-inch border from the edge farthest away from you. Top the cheese with the chicken and onion mixture, spreading it out evenly. Drizzle the cheese sauce over the meat and sprinkle the remaining Cheddar cheese on top.

4. Start rolling the stromboli away from you and toward the empty border. Make sure the filling stays tightly tucked inside the roll. Finally, tuck the ends of the dough in and pinch the seam shut. Place the seam side down and shape the Stromboli into a U-shape to fit in the air-fry basket. Cut 4 small slits with the tip of a sharp knife evenly in the top of the dough and lightly brush the stromboli with a little oil.

5. Preheat the air fryer to 370°F.

6. Spray or brush the air fryer basket with oil and transfer the U-shaped stromboli to the air

fryer basket. Air-fry for 12 minutes, turning the stromboli over halfway through the cooking time. (Use a plate to invert the stromboli out of the air fryer basket and then slide it back into the basket off the plate.)

7. To remove, carefully flip stromboli over onto a cutting board. Let it rest for a couple of minutes before serving. Slice the stromboli into 3-inch pieces and serve with ketchup for dipping, if desired.

Chicken Nuggets

Servings: 20
Cooking Time: 14 Minutes Per Batch

Ingredients:

- 1 pound boneless, skinless chicken thighs, cut into 1-inch chunks
- ¾ teaspoon salt
- ½ teaspoon black pepper
- ½ teaspoon garlic powder
- ½ teaspoon onion powder
- ½ cup flour
- 2 eggs, beaten
- ½ cup panko breadcrumbs
- 3 tablespoons plain breadcrumbs
- oil for misting or cooking spray

Directions:

1. In the bowl of a food processor, combine chicken, ½ teaspoon salt, pepper, garlic powder, and onion powder. Process in short pulses until chicken is very finely chopped and well blended.
2. Place flour in one shallow dish and beaten eggs in another. In a third dish or plastic bag, mix together the panko crumbs, plain breadcrumbs, and ¼ teaspoon salt.

3. Shape chicken mixture into small nuggets. Dip nuggets in flour, then eggs, then panko crumb mixture.
4. Spray nuggets on both sides with oil or cooking spray and place in air fryer basket in a single layer, close but not overlapping.
5. Cook at 360°F for 10minutes. Spray with oil and cook 4 minutes, until chicken is done and coating is golden brown.
6. Repeat step 5 to cook remaining nuggets.

Thai Chicken Drumsticks

Servings: 4
Cooking Time: 20 Minutes

Ingredients:

- 2 tablespoons soy sauce
- ¼ cup rice wine vinegar
- 2 tablespoons chili garlic sauce
- 2 tablespoons sesame oil
- 1 teaspoon minced fresh ginger
- 2 teaspoons sugar
- ½ teaspoon ground coriander
- juice of 1 lime
- 8 chicken drumsticks (about 2½ pounds)
- ¼ cup chopped peanuts
- chopped fresh cilantro
- lime wedges

Directions:

1. Combine the soy sauce, rice wine vinegar, chili sauce, sesame oil, ginger, sugar, coriander and lime juice in a large bowl and mix together. Add the chicken drumsticks and marinate for 30 minutes.
2. Preheat the air fryer to 370°F.
3. Place the chicken in the air fryer basket. It's ok if the ends of the drumsticks overlap a little.

Spoon half of the marinade over the chicken, and reserve the other half.

4. Air-fry for 10 minutes. Turn the chicken over and pour the rest of the marinade over the chicken. Air-fry for an additional 10 minutes.

5. Transfer the chicken to a plate to rest and cool to an edible temperature. Pour the marinade from the bottom of the air fryer into a small saucepan and bring it to a simmer over medium-high heat. Simmer the liquid for 2 minutes so that it thickens enough to coat the back of a spoon.

6. Transfer the chicken to a serving platter, pour the sauce over the chicken and sprinkle the chopped peanuts on top. Garnish with chopped cilantro and lime wedges.

Turkey-hummus Wraps

Servings: 4
Cooking Time: 7 Minutes Per Batch

Ingredients:
- 4 large whole wheat wraps
- ½ cup hummus
- 16 thin slices deli turkey
- 8 slices provolone cheese
- 1 cup fresh baby spinach (or more to taste)

Directions:
1. To assemble, place 2 tablespoons of hummus on each wrap and spread to within about a half inch from edges. Top with 4 slices of turkey and 2 slices of provolone. Finish with ¼ cup of baby spinach—or pile on as much as you like.

2. Roll up each wrap. You don't need to fold or seal the ends.

3. Place 2 wraps in air fryer basket, seam side down.

4. Cook at 360°F for 4minutes to warm filling and melt cheese. If you like, you can continue cooking for 3 more minutes, until the wrap is slightly crispy.

5. Repeat step 4 to cook remaining wraps.

Jerk Turkey Meatballs

Servings: 7
Cooking Time: 8 Minutes

Ingredients:
- 1 pound lean ground turkey
- ¼ cup chopped onion
- 1 teaspoon minced garlic
- ½ teaspoon dried thyme
- ¼ teaspoon ground cinnamon
- 1 teaspoon cayenne pepper
- ½ teaspoon paprika
- ½ teaspoon salt
- ⅛ teaspoon black pepper
- ¼ teaspoon red pepper flakes
- 2 teaspoons brown sugar
- 1 large egg, whisked
- ⅓ cup panko breadcrumbs
- 2⅓ cups cooked brown Jasmine rice
- 2 green onions, chopped
- ¾ cup sweet onion dressing

Directions:
1. Preheat the air fryer to 350°F.

2. In a medium bowl, mix the ground turkey with the onion, garlic, thyme, cinnamon, cayenne pepper, paprika, salt, pepper, red pepper flakes, and brown sugar. Add the whisked egg and stir in the breadcrumbs until the turkey starts to hold together.

3. Using a 1-ounce scoop, portion the turkey into meatballs. You should get about 28 meatballs.

4. Spray the air fryer basket with olive oil spray.

5. Place the meatballs into the air fryer basket and cook for 5 minutes, shake the basket, and cook another 2 to 4 minutes (or until the internal temperature of the meatballs reaches 165°F).

6. Remove the meatballs from the basket and repeat for the remaining meatballs.

7. Serve warm over a bed of rice with chopped green onions and spicy Caribbean jerk dressing.

Coconut Curry Chicken With Coconut Rice

Servings: 4

Cooking Time: 56 Minutes

Ingredients:

- 1 (14-ounce) can coconut milk
- 2 tablespoons green or red curry paste
- zest and juice of one lime
- 1 clove garlic, minced
- 1 tablespoon grated fresh ginger
- 1 teaspoon ground cumin
- 1 (3- to 4-pound) chicken, cut into 8 pieces
- vegetable or olive oil
- salt and freshly ground black pepper
- fresh cilantro leaves
- For the rice:
- 1 cup basmati or jasmine rice
- 1 cup water
- 1 cup coconut milk
- ½ teaspoon salt
- freshly ground black pepper

Directions:

1. Make the marinade by combining the coconut milk, curry paste, lime zest and juice, garlic, ginger and cumin. Coat the chicken on all sides with the marinade and marinate the chicken for 1 hour to overnight in the refrigerator.

2. Preheat the air fryer to 380°F.

3. Brush the bottom of the air fryer basket with oil. Transfer the chicken thighs and drumsticks from the marinade to the air fryer basket, letting most of the marinade drip off. Season to taste with salt and freshly ground black pepper.

4. Air-fry the chicken drumsticks and thighs at 380°F for 12 minutes. Flip the chicken over and continue to air-fry for another 12 minutes. Set aside and air-fry the chicken breast pieces at 380°F for 15 minutes. Turn the chicken breast pieces over and air-fry for another 12 minutes. Return the chicken thighs and drumsticks to the air fryer and air-fry for an additional 5 minutes.

5. While the chicken is cooking, make the coconut rice. Rinse the rice kernels with water and drain well. Place the rice in a medium saucepan with a tight fitting lid, along with the water, coconut milk, salt and freshly ground black pepper. Bring the mixture to a boil and then cover, reduce the heat and let it cook gently for 20 minutes without lifting the lid. When the time is up, lift the lid, fluff with a fork and set aside.

6. Remove the chicken from the air fryer and serve warm with the coconut rice and fresh cilantro scattered around.

Crispy Duck With Cherry Sauce

Servings: 2

Cooking Time: 33 Minutes

Ingredients:

- 1 whole duck (up to 5 pounds), split in half, back and rib bones removed
- 1 teaspoon olive oil
- salt and freshly ground black pepper
- Cherry Sauce:
- 1 tablespoon butter
- 1 shallot, minced

- ½ cup sherry
- ¾ cup cherry preserves 1 cup chicken stock
- 1 teaspoon white wine vinegar
- 1 teaspoon fresh thyme leaves
- salt and freshly ground black pepper

Directions:
1. Preheat the air fryer to 400°F.
2. Trim some of the fat from the duck. Rub olive oil on the duck and season with salt and pepper. Place the duck halves in the air fryer basket, breast side up and facing the center of the basket.
3. Air-fry the duck for 20 minutes. Turn the duck over and air-fry for another 6 minutes.
4. While duck is air-frying, make the cherry sauce. Melt the butter in a large sauté pan. Add the shallot and sauté until it is just starting to brown – about 2 to 3 minutes. Add the sherry and deglaze the pan by scraping up any brown bits from the bottom of the pan. Simmer the liquid for a few minutes, until it has reduced by half. Add the cherry preserves, chicken stock and white wine vinegar. Whisk well to combine all the ingredients. Simmer the sauce until it thickens and coats the back of a spoon – about 5 to 7 minutes. Season with salt and pepper and stir in the fresh thyme leaves.
5. When the air fryer timer goes off, spoon some cherry sauce over the duck and continue to air-fry at 400°F for 4 more minutes. Then, turn the duck halves back over so that the breast side is facing up. Spoon more cherry sauce over the top of the duck, covering the skin completely. Air-fry for 3 more minutes and then remove the duck to a plate to rest for a few minutes.
6. Serve the duck in halves, or cut each piece in half again for a smaller serving. Spoon any additional sauce over the duck or serve it on the side.

Teriyaki Chicken Legs

Servings: 2
Cooking Time: 20 Minutes

Ingredients:
- 4 tablespoons teriyaki sauce
- 1 tablespoon orange juice
- 1 teaspoon smoked paprika
- 4 chicken legs
- cooking spray

Directions:
1. Mix together the teriyaki sauce, orange juice, and smoked paprika. Brush on all sides of chicken legs.
2. Spray air fryer basket with nonstick cooking spray and place chicken in basket.
3. Cook at 360°F for 6minutes. Turn and baste with sauce. Cook for 6 moreminutes, turn and baste. Cook for 8 minutes more, until juices run clear when chicken is pierced with a fork.

Chicken Adobo

Servings: 6
Cooking Time: 12 Minutes

Ingredients:
- 6 boneless chicken thighs
- ¼ cup soy sauce or tamari
- ½ cup rice wine vinegar
- 4 cloves garlic, minced
- ⅛ teaspoon crushed red pepper flakes
- ½ teaspoon black pepper

Directions:
1. Place the chicken thighs into a resealable plastic bag with the soy sauce or tamari, the rice

wine vinegar, the garlic, and the crushed red pepper flakes. Seal the bag and let the chicken marinate at least 1 hour in the refrigerator.

2. Preheat the air fryer to 400°F.

3. Drain the chicken and pat dry with a paper towel. Season the chicken with black pepper and liberally spray with cooking spray.

4. Place the chicken in the air fryer basket and cook for 9 minutes, turn over at 9 minutes and check for an internal temperature of 165°F, and cook another 3 minutes.

Nacho Chicken Fries

Servings: 4
Cooking Time: 7 Minutes

Ingredients:

- 1 pound chicken tenders
- salt
- ¼ cup flour
- 2 eggs
- ¾ cup panko breadcrumbs
- ¾ cup crushed organic nacho cheese tortilla chips
- oil for misting or cooking spray
- Seasoning Mix
- 1 tablespoon chili powder
- 1 teaspoon ground cumin
- ½ teaspoon garlic powder
- ½ teaspoon onion powder

Directions:

1. Stir together all seasonings in a small cup and set aside.

2. Cut chicken tenders in half crosswise, then cut into strips no wider than about ½ inch.

3. Preheat air fryer to 390°F.

4. Salt chicken to taste. Place strips in large bowl and sprinkle with 1 tablespoon of the seasoning mix. Stir well to distribute seasonings.

5. Add flour to chicken and stir well to coat all sides.

6. Beat eggs together in a shallow dish.

7. In a second shallow dish, combine the panko, crushed chips, and the remaining 2 teaspoons of seasoning mix.

8. Dip chicken strips in eggs, then roll in crumbs. Mist with oil or cooking spray.

9. Chicken strips will cook best if done in two batches. They can be crowded and overlapping a little but not stacked in double or triple layers.

10. Cook for 4minutes. Shake basket, mist with oil, and cook 3 moreminutes, until chicken juices run clear and outside is crispy.

11. Repeat step 10 to cook remaining chicken fries.

Chicken Rochambeau

Servings: 4
Cooking Time: 20 Minutes

Ingredients:

- 1 tablespoon butter
- 4 chicken tenders, cut in half crosswise
- salt and pepper
- ¼ cup flour
- oil for misting
- 4 slices ham, ¼- to ⅜-inches thick and large enough to cover an English muffin
- 2 English muffins, split
- Sauce
- 2 tablespoons butter
- ½ cup chopped green onions
- ½ cup chopped mushrooms
- 2 tablespoons flour

- 1 cup chicken broth
- ¼ teaspoon garlic powder
- 1½ teaspoons Worcestershire sauce

Directions:

1. Place 1 tablespoon of butter in air fryer baking pan and cook at 390°F for 2minutes to melt.

2. Sprinkle chicken tenders with salt and pepper to taste, then roll in the ¼ cup of flour.

3. Place chicken in baking pan, turning pieces to coat with melted butter.

4. Cook at 390°F for 5minutes. Turn chicken pieces over, and spray tops lightly with olive oil. Cook 5minutes longer or until juices run clear. The chicken will not brown.

5. While chicken is cooking, make the sauce: In a medium saucepan, melt the 2 tablespoons of butter.

6. Add onions and mushrooms and sauté until tender, about 3minutes.

7. Stir in the flour. Gradually add broth, stirring constantly until you have a smooth gravy.

8. Add garlic powder and Worcestershire sauce and simmer on low heat until sauce thickens, about 5minutes.

9. When chicken is cooked, remove baking pan from air fryer and set aside.

10. Place ham slices directly into air fryer basket and cook at 390°F for 5minutes or until hot and beginning to sizzle a little. Remove and set aside on top of the chicken for now.

11. Place the English muffin halves in air fryer basket and cook at 390°F for 1 minute.

12. Open air fryer and place a ham slice on top of each English muffin half. Stack 2 pieces of chicken on top of each ham slice. Cook at 390°F for 1 to 2minutes to heat through.

13. Place each English muffin stack on a serving plate and top with plenty of sauce.

Appetizers And Snacks

Shrimp Pirogues

Servings: 8

Cooking Time: 5 Minutes

Ingredients:

- 12 ounces small, peeled, and deveined raw shrimp
- 3 ounces cream cheese, room temperature
- 2 tablespoons plain yogurt
- 1 teaspoon lemon juice
- 1 teaspoon dried dill weed, crushed
- salt
- 4 small hothouse cucumbers, each approximately 6 inches long

Directions:

1. Pour 4 tablespoons water in bottom of air fryer drawer.

2. Place shrimp in air fryer basket in single layer and cook at 390°F for 5 minutes, just until done. Watch carefully because shrimp cooks quickly, and overcooking makes it tough.

3. Chop shrimp into small pieces, no larger than ½ inch. Refrigerate while mixing the remaining ingredients.

4. With a fork, mash and whip the cream cheese until smooth.

5. Stir in the yogurt and beat until smooth. Stir in lemon juice, dill weed, and chopped shrimp.

6. Taste for seasoning. If needed, add ¼ to ½ teaspoon salt to suit your taste.

7. Store in refrigerator until serving time.

8. When ready to serve, wash and dry cucumbers and split them lengthwise. Scoop out the seeds and turn cucumbers upside down on paper towels to drain for 10minutes.

9. Just before filling, wipe centers of cucumbers dry. Spoon the shrimp mixture into the pirogues and cut in half crosswise. Serve immediately.

Fiery Bacon-wrapped Dates

Servings: 16

Cooking Time: 6 Minutes

Ingredients:

- 8 Thin-cut bacon strips, halved widthwise (gluten-free, if a concern)
- 16 Medium or large Medjool dates, pitted
- 3 tablespoons (about ¾ ounce) Shredded semi-firm mozzarella
- 32 Pickled jalapeño rings

Directions:

1. Preheat the air fryer to 400°F.

2. Lay a bacon strip half on a clean, dry work surface. Split one date lengthwise without cutting through it, so that it opens like a pocket. Set it on one end of the bacon strip and open it a bit. Place 1 teaspoon of the shredded cheese and 2 pickled jalapeño rings in the date, then gently squeeze it together without fully closing it (just to hold the stuffing inside). Roll up the date in the bacon strip and set it bacon seam side down on a cutting board. Repeat this process with the remaining bacon strip halves, dates, cheese, and jalapeño rings.

3. Place the bacon-wrapped dates bacon seam side down in the basket. Air-fry undisturbed for 6 minutes, or until crisp and brown.

4. Use kitchen tongs to gently transfer the wrapped dates to a wire rack or serving platter. Cool for a few minutes before serving.

Green Olive And Mushroom Tapenade

Servings: 1

Cooking Time: 10 Minutes

Ingredients:

- ¾ pound Brown or Baby Bella mushrooms, sliced
- 1½ cups (about ½ pound) Pitted green olives
- 3 tablespoons Olive oil
- 1½ tablespoons Fresh oregano leaves, loosely packed
- ¼ teaspoon Ground black pepper

Directions:

1. Preheat the air fryer to 400°F.

2. When the machine is at temperature, arrange the mushroom slices in as close to an even layer as possible in the basket. They will overlap and even stack on top of each other.

3. Air-fry for 10 minutes, tossing the basket and rearranging the mushrooms every 2 minutes, until shriveled but with still-noticeable moisture.

4. Pour the mushrooms into a food processor. Add the olives, olive oil, oregano leaves, and pepper. Cover and process until grainy, not too much, just not fully smooth for better texture, stopping the machine at least once to scrape down the inside of the canister. Scrape the tapenade into a bowl and serve warm, or cover and refrigerate for up to 4 days. (The tapenade will taste better if it comes back to room temperature before serving.)

Cauliflower-crust Pizza

Servings: 3

Cooking Time: 14 Minutes

Ingredients:

- 1 pound 2 ounces Riced cauliflower
- 1 plus 1 large egg yolk Large egg(s)
- 3 tablespoons (a little more than ½ ounce) Finely grated Parmesan cheese
- 1½ tablespoons Potato starch
- ¾ teaspoon Dried oregano
- ¾ teaspoon Table salt
- Vegetable oil spray
- 3 tablespoons Purchased pizza sauce
- 6 tablespoons (about 1½ ounces) Shredded semi-firm mozzarella

Directions:

1. Pour the riced cauliflower into a medium microwave-safe bowl. Microwave on high for 4 minutes. Stir well, then cool for 15 minutes.

2. Preheat the air fryer to 400°F.

3. Pour the riced cauliflower into a clean kitchen towel or a large piece of cheesecloth. Gather the towel or cheesecloth together. Working over the sink, squeeze the moisture out of the cauliflower, getting out as much of the liquid as you can.

4. Pour the squeezed cauliflower back into that same medium bowl and stir in the egg, egg yolk (if using), cheese, potato starch, oregano, and salt to form a loose, uniform "dough."

5. Cut a piece of aluminum foil or parchment paper into a 6-inch circle for a small pizza, a 7-inch circle for a medium one, or an 8-inch circle for a large one. Coat the circle with vegetable oil spray, then place it in the air-fryer basket. Using a small offset spatula or the back of a flatware tablespoon, spread and smooth the cauliflower mixture onto the circle right to the edges. Air-fry undisturbed for 10 minutes.

6. Remove the basket from the air fryer. Reduce the machine's temperature to 350°F .

7. Using a large nonstick-safe spatula, flip over the cauliflower circle along with its foil or parchment paper right in the basket. Peel off and discard the foil or parchment paper. Spread the pizza sauce evenly over the crust and sprinkle with the cheese.

8. Air-fry undisturbed for 4 minutes, or until the cheese has melted and begun to bubble. Remove the basket from the machine and cool for 5 minutes. Use the same spatula to transfer the pizza to a wire rack to cool for 5 minutes more before cutting the pie into wedges to serve.

Honey-mustard Chicken Wings

Servings: 2

Cooking Time: 14 Minutes

Ingredients:

- 2 pounds chicken wings
- salt and freshly ground black pepper
- 2 tablespoons butter
- ¼ cup honey
- ¼ cup spicy brown mustard
- pinch ground cayenne pepper
- 2 teaspoons Worcestershire sauce

Directions:

1. Prepare the chicken wings by cutting off the wing tips and discarding (or freezing for chicken stock). Divide the drumettes from the wingettes by cutting through the joint. Place the chicken wing pieces in a large bowl.

2. Preheat the air fryer to 400°F.

3. Season the wings with salt and freshly ground black pepper and air-fry the wings in two batches for 10 minutes per batch, shaking the basket half way through the cooking process.

4. While the wings are air-frying, combine the remaining ingredients in a small saucepan over low heat.

5. When both batches are done, toss all the wings with the honey-mustard sauce and toss them all back into the basket for another 4 minutes to heat through and finish cooking. Give the basket a good shake part way through the cooking process to redistribute the wings. Remove the wings from the air fryer and serve.

Vegetable Spring Rolls

Servings: 6

Cooking Time: 8 Minutes

Ingredients:

- ¾ cup (a little more than 2½ ounces) Fresh bean sprouts
- 6 tablespoons Shredded carrots
- 6 tablespoons Slivered, drained, sliced canned bamboo shoots
- 1½ tablespoons Regular or low-sodium soy sauce or gluten-free tamari sauce
- 1½ teaspoons Granulated white sugar
- 1½ teaspoons Toasted sesame oil
- 6 Spring roll wrappers (gluten-free, if a concern)
- 1 Large egg, well beaten
- Vegetable oil spray

Directions:

1. Gently stir the bean sprouts, carrots, bamboo shoots, soy or tamari sauce, sugar, and oil in a large bowl until the vegetables are evenly coated. Set aside at room temperature for 10 to 15 minutes.

2. Preheat the air fryer to 400°F.

3. Set a spring roll wrapper on a clean, dry work surface. Pick up about ¼ cup of the vegetable

mixture and gently squeeze it in your clean hand to release most of the liquid. Set this bundle of vegetables along one edge of the wrapper.

4. Fold two opposing sides (at right angles to the filling) up and over the filling, concealing part of it and making a folded-over border down two sides of the wrapper. Brush the top half of the wrapper (including the folded parts) with beaten egg so it will seal when you roll it closed.

5. Starting with the side nearest the filling, roll the wrapper closed, working to make a tight fit, eliminating as much air as possible from inside the wrapper. Set it aside seam side down and continue making more filled rolls using the same techniques.

6. Lightly coat all the sealed rolls with vegetable oil spray on all sides. Set them seam side down in the basket and air-fry undisturbed for 8 minutes, or until golden brown and very crisp.

7. Use a nonstick-safe spatula and a flatware fork for balance to transfer the rolls to a wire rack. Cool for at least 5 minutes or up to 15 minutes before serving.

Italian Rice Balls

Servings: 8
Cooking Time: 10 Minutes

Ingredients:

- 1½ cups cooked sticky rice
- ½ teaspoon Italian seasoning blend
- ¾ teaspoon salt
- 8 pitted black olives
- 1 ounce mozzarella cheese cut into tiny sticks (small enough to stuff into olives)
- 2 eggs, beaten
- ⅓ cup Italian breadcrumbs
- ¾ cup panko breadcrumbs

- oil for misting or cooking spray

Directions:

1. Preheat air fryer to 390°F.
2. Stir together the cooked rice, Italian seasoning, and ½ teaspoon of salt.
3. Stuff each black olive with a piece of mozzarella cheese.
4. Shape the rice into a log and divide into 8 equal pieces. Using slightly damp hands, mold each portion of rice around an olive and shape into a firm ball. Chill in freezer for 10 to 15minutes or until the outside is cold to the touch.
5. Set up 3 shallow dishes for dipping: beaten eggs in one dish, Italian breadcrumbs in another dish, and in the third dish mix the panko crumbs and remaining salt.
6. Roll each rice ball in breadcrumbs, dip in beaten egg, and then roll in the panko crumbs.
7. Spray all sides with oil.
8. Cook for 10minutes, until outside is light golden brown and crispy.

Fried Dill Pickle Chips

Servings: 4
Cooking Time: 12 Minutes

Ingredients:

- 1 cup All-purpose flour or tapioca flour
- 1 Large egg white(s)
- 1 tablespoon Brine from a jar of dill pickles
- 1 cup Seasoned Italian-style dried bread crumbs (gluten-free, if a concern)
- 2 Large dill pickle(s) (8 to 10 inches long), cut into ½-inch-thick rounds
- Vegetable oil spray

Directions:

1. Preheat the air fryer to 400°F.

2. Set up and fill three shallow soup plates or small pie plates on your counter: one for the flour, one for the egg white(s) whisked with the pickle brine, and one for the bread crumbs.

3. Set a pickle round in the flour and turn it to coat all sides, even the edge. Gently shake off the excess flour, then dip the round into the egg-white mixture and turn to coat both sides and the edge. Let any excess egg white mixture slip back into the rest, then set the round in the bread crumbs and turn it to coat both sides as well as the edge. Set aside on a cutting board and soldier on, dipping and coating the remaining rounds. Lightly coat the coated rounds on both sides with vegetable oil spray.

4. Set the pickle rounds in the basket in one layer. Air-fry undisturbed for 7 minutes, or until golden brown and crunchy. Cool in the basket for a few minutes before using kitchen tongs to transfer the (still hot) rounds to a serving platter.

Turkey Burger Sliders

Servings: 8
Cooking Time: 7 Minutes

Ingredients:

- 1 pound ground turkey
- ¼ teaspoon curry powder
- 1 teaspoon Hoisin sauce
- ½ teaspoon salt
- 8 slider buns
- ½ cup slivered red onions
- ½ cup slivered green or red bell pepper
- ½ cup fresh chopped pineapple (or pineapple tidbits from kids' fruit cups, drained)
- light cream cheese, softened

Directions:

1. Combine turkey, curry powder, Hoisin sauce, and salt and mix together well.

2. Shape turkey mixture into 8 small patties.

3. Place patties in air fryer basket and cook at 360°F for 7minutes, until patties are well done and juices run clear.

4. Place each patty on the bottom half of a slider bun and top with onions, peppers, and pineapple. Spread the remaining bun halves with cream cheese to taste, place on top, and serve.

Charred Shishito Peppers

Servings: 4
Cooking Time: 5 Minutes

Ingredients:

- 20 shishito peppers (about 6 ounces)
- 1 teaspoon vegetable oil
- coarse sea salt
- 1 lemon

Directions:

1. Preheat the air fryer to 390°F.

2. Toss the shishito peppers with the oil and salt. You can do this in a bowl or directly in the air fryer basket.

3. Air-fry at 390°F for 5 minutes, shaking the basket once or twice while they cook.

4. Turn the charred peppers out into a bowl. Squeeze some lemon juice over the top and season with coarse sea salt. These should be served as finger foods – pick the pepper up by the stem and eat the whole pepper, seeds and all. Watch for that surprise spicy one!

Poutine

Servings: 2
Cooking Time: 25 Minutes

Ingredients:

- 2 russet potatoes, scrubbed and cut into ½-inch sticks
- 2 teaspoons vegetable oil
- 2 tablespoons butter
- ¼ onion, minced (about ¼ cup)
- 1 clove garlic, smashed
- ¼ teaspoon dried thyme
- 3 tablespoons flour
- 1 teaspoon tomato paste
- 1½ cups strong beef stock
- salt and lots of freshly ground black pepper
- a few dashes of Worcestershire sauce
- ⅔ cup chopped string cheese or cheese curds

Directions:

1. Bring a large saucepan of salted water to a boil on the stovetop while you peel and cut the potatoes. Blanch the potatoes in the boiling salted water for 4 minutes while you Preheat the air fryer to 400°F. Strain the potatoes and rinse them with cold water. Dry them well with a clean kitchen towel.

2. Toss the dried potato sticks gently with the oil and place them in the air fryer basket. Air-fry for 25 minutes, shaking the basket a few times while the fries cook to help them brown evenly.

3. While the fries are cooking, make the gravy. Melt the butter in a small saucepan over medium heat. Add the onion, garlic and thyme and cook for five minutes, until soft and just starting to brown. Stir in the flour and cook for another two minutes, stirring regularly. Finally, add the tomato paste and continue to cook for another minute or two. Whisk in the beef stock and bring the mixture to a boil to thicken. Season to taste with salt, lots of freshly ground black pepper and a few dashes of Worcestershire sauce. Keep the gravy warm.

4. As soon as the fries are done, season them with salt and transfer to a plate or basket. Top the fries with the cheese curds or string cheese, and pour the warm gravy over the top.

Skinny Fries

Servings: 2
Cooking Time: 15 Minutes

Ingredients:

- 2 to 3 russet potatoes, peeled and cut into ¼-inch sticks
- 2 to 3 teaspoons olive or vegetable oil
- salt

Directions:

1. Cut the potatoes into ¼-inch strips. (A mandolin with a julienne blade is really helpful here.) Rinse the potatoes with cold water several times and let them soak in cold water for at least 10 minutes or as long as overnight.

2. Preheat the air fryer to 380°F.

3. Drain and dry the potato sticks really well, using a clean kitchen towel. Toss the fries with the oil in a bowl and then air-fry the fries in two batches at 380°F for 15 minutes, shaking the basket a couple of times while they cook.

4. Add the first batch of French fries back into the air fryer basket with the finishing batch and let everything warm through for a few minutes. As soon as the fries are done, season them with salt and transfer to a plate or basket. Serve them warm with ketchup or your favorite dip.

Antipasto-stuffed Cherry Tomatoes

Servings: 12
Cooking Time: 9 Minutes

Ingredients:

- 12 Large cherry tomatoes, preferably Campari tomatoes (about 1½ ounces each and the size of golf balls)
- ½ cup Seasoned Italian-style dried bread crumbs (gluten-free, if a concern)
- ¼ cup (about ¾ ounce) Finely grated Parmesan cheese
- ¼ cup Finely chopped pitted black olives
- ¼ cup Finely chopped marinated artichoke hearts
- 2 tablespoons Marinade from the artichokes
- 4 Sun-dried tomatoes (dry, not packed in oil), finely chopped
- Olive oil spray

Directions:

1. Preheat the air fryer to 400°F.
2. Cut the top off of each fresh tomato, exposing the seeds and pulp. (The tops can be saved for a snack, sprinkled with some kosher salt, to tide you over while the stuffed tomatoes cook.) Cut a very small slice off the bottom of each tomato (no cutting into the pulp) so it will stand up flat on your work surface. Use a melon baller to remove and discard the seeds and pulp from each tomato.
3. Mix the bread crumbs, cheese, olives, artichoke hearts, marinade, and sun-dried tomatoes in a bowl until well combined. Stuff this mixture into each prepared tomato, about 1½ tablespoons in each. Generously coat the tops of the tomatoes with olive oil spray.
4. Set the tomatoes stuffing side up in the basket. Air-fry undisturbed for 9 minutes, or until the stuffing has browned a bit and the tomatoes are blistered in places.
5. Remove the basket and cool the tomatoes in it for 5 minutes. Then use kitchen tongs to gently transfer the tomatoes to a serving platter.

Sweet Apple Fries

Servings: 3
Cooking Time: 8 Minutes

Ingredients:

- 2 Medium-size sweet apple(s), such as Gala or Fuji
- 1 Large egg white(s)
- 2 tablespoons Water
- 1½ cups Finely ground gingersnap crumbs (gluten-free, if a concern)
- Vegetable oil spray

Directions:

1. Preheat the air fryer to 375°F .
2. Peel and core an apple, then cut it into 12 slices (see the headnote for more information). Repeat with more apples as necessary.
3. Whisk the egg white(s) and water in a medium bowl until foamy. Add the apple slices and toss well to coat.
4. Spread the gingersnap crumbs across a dinner plate. Using clean hands, pick up an apple slice, let any excess egg white mixture slip back into the rest, and dredge the slice in the crumbs, coating it lightly but evenly on all sides. Set it aside and continue coating the remaining apple slices.
5. Lightly coat the slices on all sides with vegetable oil spray, then set them curved side down in the basket in one layer. Air-fry undisturbed for 6 minutes, or until browned and crisp. You may need to air-fry the slices for 2 minutes longer if the temperature is at 360°F.

6. Use kitchen tongs to transfer the slices to a wire rack. Cool for 2 to 3 minutes before serving.

Fried Green Tomatoes

Servings: 4

Cooking Time: 15 Minutes

Ingredients:

- 2 eggs
- ¼ cup buttermilk
- ½ cup cornmeal
- ½ cup breadcrumbs
- ¼ teaspoon salt
- 1½ pounds firm green tomatoes, cut in ¼-inch slices
- oil for misting or cooking spray
- Horseradish Drizzle
- ¼ cup mayonnaise
- ¼ cup sour cream
- 2 teaspoons prepared horseradish
- ½ teaspoon Worcestershire sauce
- ½ teaspoon lemon juice
- ⅛ teaspoon black pepper

Directions:

1. Mix all ingredients for Horseradish Drizzle together and chill while you prepare the green tomatoes.

2. Preheat air fryer to 390°F.

3. Beat the eggs and buttermilk together in a shallow bowl.

4. Mix cornmeal, breadcrumbs, and salt together in a plate or shallow dish.

5. Dip 4 tomato slices in the egg mixture, then roll in the breadcrumb mixture.

6. Mist one side with oil and place in air fryer basket, oil-side down, in a single layer.

7. Mist the top with oil.

8. Cook for 15minutes, turning once, until brown and crispy.

9. Repeat steps 5 through 8 to cook remaining tomatoes.

10. Drizzle horseradish sauce over tomatoes just before serving.

Shrimp Egg Rolls

Servings: 8

Cooking Time: 10 Minutes

Ingredients:

- 1 tablespoon vegetable oil
- ½ head green or savoy cabbage, finely shredded
- 1 cup shredded carrots
- 1 cup canned bean sprouts, drained
- 1 tablespoon soy sauce
- ½ teaspoon sugar
- 1 teaspoon sesame oil
- ¼ cup hoisin sauce
- freshly ground black pepper
- 1 pound cooked shrimp, diced
- ¼ cup scallions
- 8 egg roll wrappers
- vegetable oil
- duck sauce

Directions:

1. Preheat a large sauté pan over medium-high heat. Add the oil and cook the cabbage, carrots and bean sprouts until they start to wilt – about 3 minutes. Add the soy sauce, sugar, sesame oil, hoisin sauce and black pepper. Sauté for a few more minutes. Stir in the shrimp and scallions and cook until the vegetables are just tender. Transfer the mixture to a colander in a bowl to cool. Press or squeeze out any excess water from

the filling so that you don't end up with soggy egg rolls.

2. To make the egg rolls, place the egg roll wrappers on a flat surface with one of the points facing towards you so they look like diamonds. Dividing the filling evenly between the eight wrappers, spoon the mixture onto the center of the egg roll wrappers. Spread the filling across the center of the wrappers from the left corner to the right corner, but leave 2 inches from each corner empty. Brush the empty sides of the wrapper with a little water. Fold the bottom corner of the wrapper tightly up over the filling, trying to avoid making any air pockets. Fold the left corner in toward the center and then the right corner toward the center. It should now look like an envelope. Tightly roll the egg roll from the bottom to the top open corner. Press to seal the egg roll together, brushing with a little extra water if need be. Repeat this technique with all 8 egg rolls.

3. Preheat the air fryer to 370°F.

4. Spray or brush all sides of the egg rolls with vegetable oil. Air-fry four egg rolls at a time for 10 minutes, turning them over halfway through the cooking time.

5. Serve hot with duck sauce or your favorite dipping sauce.

Pita Chips

Servings: 4
Cooking Time: 10 Minutes

Ingredients:
- 2 rounds Pocketless pita bread
- Olive oil spray or any flavor spray you prefer, even coconut oil spray
- Up to 1 teaspoon Fine sea salt, garlic salt, onion salt, or other flavored salt

Directions:
1. Preheat the air fryer to 400°F.
2. Lightly coat the pita round(s) on both sides with olive oil spray, then lightly sprinkle each side with salt.
3. Cut each coated pita round into 8 even wedges. Lay these in the basket in as close to a single even layer as possible. Many will overlap or even be on top of each other, depending on the exact size of your machine.
4. Air-fry for 6 minutes, shaking the basket and rearranging the wedges at the 4-minute marks, until the wedges are crisp and brown. Turn them out onto a wire rack to cool a few minutes or to room temperature before digging in.

Sausage And Cheese Rolls

Servings: 3
Cooking Time: 18 Minutes

Ingredients:
- 3 3- to 3½-ounce sweet or hot Italian sausage links
- 2 1-ounce string cheese stick(s), unwrapped and cut in half lengthwise
- Three quarters from one thawed sheet (cut the sheet into four quarters; wrap and refreeze one of them) A 17.25-ounce box frozen puff pastry

Directions:
1. Preheat the air fryer to 400°F.
2. When the machine is at temperature, set the sausage links in the basket and air-fry undisturbed for 12 minutes, or until cooked through.
3. Use kitchen tongs to transfer the links to a wire rack. Cool for 15 minutes. (If necessary,

pour out any rendered fat that has collected below the basket in the machine.)

4. Cut the sausage links in half lengthwise. Sandwich half a string cheese stick between two sausage halves, trimming the ends so the cheese doesn't stick out beyond the meat.

5. Roll each piece of puff pastry into a 6 x 6-inch square on a clean, dry work surface. Set the sausage-cheese sandwich at one edge and roll it up in the dough. The ends will be open like a pig-in-a-blanket. Repeat with the remaining puff pastry, sausage, and cheese.

6. Set the rolls seam side down in the basket. Air-fry undisturbed for 6 minutes, or until puffed and golden brown.

7. Use a nonstick-safe spatula, and perhaps a flatware fork for balance, to transfer the rolls to a wire rack. Cool for at least 5 minutes before serving.

Country Wings

Servings: 4

Cooking Time: 19 Minutes

Ingredients:
- 2 pounds chicken wings
- Marinade
- 1 cup buttermilk
- ½ teaspoon black pepper
- ½ teaspoon salt
- Coating
- 1 cup flour
- 1 cup panko breadcrumbs
- 2 teaspoons salt
- 2 tablespoons poultry seasoning
- oil for misting or cooking spray

Directions:

1. Cut the tips off the wings. Discard or freeze for stock. Cut remaining wing sections apart at the joint to make 2 pieces per wing. Place wings in a large bowl or plastic bag.

2. Mix together all marinade ingredients and pour over wings. Refrigerate for at least 1 hour but for no more than 8 hours.

3. Preheat air fryer to 360°F.

4. Mix all coating ingredients together in a shallow dish or on wax paper.

5. Remove wings from marinade, shaking off excess, and roll in coating mixture.

6. Spray both sides of each wing with oil or cooking spray.

7. Place wings in air fryer basket in single layer, close but not too crowded. Cook for 19minutes or until chicken is done and juices run clear.

8. Repeat step 7 to cook remaining wings.

Crab Toasts

Servings: 15

Cooking Time: 5 Minutes

Ingredients:
- 1 6-ounce can flaked crabmeat, well drained
- 3 tablespoons light mayonnaise
- ½ teaspoon lemon juice
- 1 teaspoon Worcestershire sauce
- ¼ cup shredded sharp Cheddar cheese
- ¼ cup shredded Parmesan cheese
- 1 loaf artisan bread, French bread, or baguette, cut into slices ⅜-inch thick

Directions:

1. Mix together all ingredients except the bread slices.

2. Spread each slice of bread with a thin layer of crabmeat mixture. (For a bread slice measuring 2

x 1½ inches you will need about ½ tablespoon of crab mixture.)

3. Place in air fryer basket in single layer and cook at 360°F for 5minutes or until tops brown and toast is crispy.

4. Repeat step 3 to cook remaining crab toasts.

Potato Samosas

Servings: 12
Cooking Time: 10 Minutes

Ingredients:

- ¾ cup Instant mashed potato flakes
- ¾ cup Boiling water
- ⅓ cup Plain full-fat or low-fat yogurt (not Greek yogurt or fat-free yogurt)
- 1 teaspoon Yellow curry powder, purchased or homemade (see here)
- ½ teaspoon Table salt
- 1½ Purchased refrigerated pie crust(s), from a minimum 14.1-ounce box
- All-purpose flour
- Vegetable oil spray

Directions:

1. Put the potato flakes in a medium bowl and pour the boiling water over them. Stir well to form a mixture like thick mashed potatoes. Cool for 15 minutes.

2. Preheat the air fryer to 400°F.

3. Stir the yogurt, curry powder, and salt into the potato mixture until smooth and uniform.

4. Unwrap and unroll the sheet(s) of pie crust dough onto a clean, dry work surface. Cut out as many 4-inch circles as you can with a big cookie cutter or a giant sturdy water glass, or even by tracing the circle with the rim of a 4-inch plate. Gather up the scraps of dough. Lightly flour your work surface and set the scraps on top. Roll them together into a sheet that matches the thickness of the original crusts and cut more circles until you have the number you need—8 circles for the small batch, 12 for the medium batch, or 16 for the large.

5. Pick up one of the circles and create something like an ice cream cone by folding and sealing the circle together so that it is closed at the bottom and flared open at the top, in a conical shape. Put 1 tablespoon of the potato filling into the open cone, then push the filling into the cone toward the point. Fold the top over the filling and press to seal the dough into a triangular shape with corners, taking care to seal those corners all around. Set aside and continue forming and filling the remainder of the dough circles as directed.

6. Lightly coat the filled dough pockets with vegetable oil spray on all sides. Set them in the basket in one layer and air-fry undisturbed for 10 minutes, or until lightly browned and crisp.

7. Gently turn the contents of the basket out onto a wire rack. Use kitchen tongs to gently set all the samosas seam side up. Cool for 10 minutes before serving.

Buffalo Bites

Servings: 16

Cooking Time: 12 Minutes

Ingredients:

- 1 pound ground chicken
- 8 tablespoons buffalo wing sauce
- 2 ounces Gruyère cheese, cut into 16 cubes
- 1 tablespoon maple syrup

Directions:

1. Mix 4 tablespoons buffalo wing sauce into all the ground chicken.

2. Shape chicken into a log and divide into 16 equal portions.

3. With slightly damp hands, mold each chicken portion around a cube of cheese and shape into a firm ball. When you have shaped 8 meatballs, place them in air fryer basket.

4. Cook at 390°F for approximately 5minutes. Shake basket, reduce temperature to 360°F, and cook for 5 minutes longer.

5. While the first batch is cooking, shape remaining chicken and cheese into 8 more meatballs.

6. Repeat step 4 to cook second batch of meatballs.

7. In a medium bowl, mix the remaining 4 tablespoons of buffalo wing sauce with the maple syrup. Add all the cooked meatballs and toss to coat.

8. Place meatballs back into air fryer basket and cook at 390°F for 2 minutes to set the glaze. Skewer each with a toothpick and serve.

Crunchy Tortellini Bites

Servings: 5

Cooking Time: 10 Minutes

Ingredients:

- 10 ounces (about 2½ cups) Cheese tortellini
- ⅓ cup Yellow cornmeal
- ⅓ cup Seasoned Italian-style dried bread crumbs
- ⅓ cup (about 1 ounce) Finely grated Parmesan cheese
- 1 Large egg
- Olive oil spray

Directions:

1. Bring a large pot of water to a boil over high heat. Add the tortellini and cook for 3 minutes. Drain in a colander set in the sink, then spread out the tortellini on a large baking sheet and cool for 15 minutes.

2. Preheat the air fryer to 400°F.

3. Mix the cornmeal, bread crumbs, and cheese in a large zip-closed plastic bag.

4. Whisk the egg in a medium bowl until uniform. Add the tortellini and toss well to coat, even along the inside curve of the pasta. Use a slotted spoon or kitchen tongs to transfer 5 or 6 tortellini to the plastic bag, seal, and shake gently to coat thoroughly and evenly. Set the coated tortellini aside on a cutting board and continue coating the rest in the same way.

5. Generously coat the tortellini on all sides with the olive oil spray, then set them in one layer in the basket. Air-fry undisturbed for 10 minutes, gently tossing the basket and rearranging the tortellini at the 4- and 7-minute marks, until brown and crisp.

6. Pour the contents of the basket onto a wire rack. Cool for 5 minutes before serving.

Vegetable Side Dishes Recipes

Home Fries

Servings: 4
Cooking Time: 20 Minutes

Ingredients:

- 3 pounds potatoes, cut into 1-inch cubes
- ½ teaspoon oil
- salt and pepper

Directions:

1. In a large bowl, mix the potatoes and oil thoroughly.
2. Cook at 390°F for 10minutes and shake the basket to redistribute potatoes.
3. Cook for an additional 10 minutes, until brown and crisp.
4. Season with salt and pepper to taste.

Cheesy Potato Skins

Servings: 6
Cooking Time: 54 Minutes

Ingredients:

- 3 6- to 8-ounce small russet potatoes
- 3 Thick-cut bacon strips, halved widthwise (gluten-free, if a concern)
- ¾ teaspoon Mild paprika
- ¼ teaspoon Garlic powder
- ¼ teaspoon Table salt
- ¼ teaspoon Ground black pepper
- ½ cup plus 1 tablespoon (a little over 2 ounces) Shredded Cheddar cheese
- 3 tablespoons Thinly sliced trimmed chives
- 6 tablespoons (a little over 1 ounce) Finely grated Parmesan cheese

Directions:

1. Preheat the air fryer to 375°F .
2. Prick each potato in four places with a fork (not four places in a line but four places all around the potato). Set the potatoes in the basket with as much air space between them as possible. Air-fry undisturbed for 45 minutes, or until the potatoes are tender when pricked with a fork.
3. Use kitchen tongs to gently transfer the potatoes to a wire rack. Cool for 15 minutes. Maintain the machine's temperature.
4. Lay the bacon strip halves in the basket in one layer. They may touch but should not overlap. Air-fry undisturbed for 5 minutes, until crisp. Use those same tongs to transfer the bacon pieces to the wire rack. If there's a great deal of rendered bacon fat in the basket's bottom or on a tray under the basket attachment, pour this into a bowl, cool, and discard. Don't throw it down the drain!
5. Cut the potatoes in half lengthwise (not just slit them open but actually cut in half). Use a flatware spoon to scoop the hot, soft middles into a bowl, leaving ½ inch of potato all around the inside of the spud next to the skin. Sprinkle the inside of the potato "shells" evenly with paprika, garlic powder, salt, and pepper.
6. Chop the bacon pieces into small bits. Sprinkle these along with the Cheddar and chives evenly inside the potato shells. Crumble 2 to 3 tablespoons of the soft potato insides over the filling mixture. Divide the grated Parmesan evenly over the tops of the potatoes.
7. Set the stuffed potatoes in the basket with as much air space between them as possible. Air-fry undisturbed for 4 minutes, until the cheese melts and lightly browns.

8. Use kitchen tongs to gently transfer the stuffed potato halves to a wire rack. Cool for 5 minutes before serving.

Hush Puppies

Servings: 8

Cooking Time: 11 Minutes

Ingredients:

- ½ cup Whole or low-fat milk (not fat-free)
- 1½ tablespoons Butter
- ½ cup plus 1 tablespoon, plus more All-purpose flour
- ½ cup plus 1 tablespoon Yellow cornmeal
- 2 teaspoons Granulated white sugar
- 2 teaspoons Baking powder
- ¾ teaspoon Baking soda
- ¾ teaspoon Table salt
- ¼ teaspoon Onion powder
- 3 tablespoons (or 1 medium egg, well beaten) Pasteurized egg substitute, such as Egg Beaters
- Vegetable oil spray

Directions:

1. Heat the milk and butter in a small saucepan set over medium heat just until the butter melts and the milk is steamy. Do not simmer or boil.

2. Meanwhile, whisk the flour, cornmeal, sugar, baking powder, baking soda, salt, and onion powder in a large bowl until the mixture is a uniform color.

3. Stir the hot milk mixture into the flour mixture to form a dough. Set aside to cool for 5 minutes.

4. Mix the egg substitute or egg into the dough to make a thick, smooth batter. Cover and refrigerate for at least 1 hour or up to 4 hours.

5. Preheat the air fryer to 350°F .

6. Lightly flour your clean, dry hands. Roll 2 tablespoons of the batter into a ball between your floured palms. Set aside, flour your hands again if necessary, and continue making more balls with the remaining batter.

7. Coat the balls all over with the vegetable oil spray. Line the machine's basket (or basket attachment) with a piece of parchment paper. Set the balls on the parchment paper with as much air space between them as possible. Air-fry for 9 minutes, or until lightly browned and set.

8. Use kitchen tongs to gently transfer the hush puppies to a wire rack. Cool for at least 5 minutes before serving. Or cool to room temperature, about 45 minutes, and store in a sealed container at room temperature for up to 2 days. To crisp the hush puppies again, put them in a 350°F air fryer for 2 minutes. (There's no need for parchment paper in the machine during reheating.)

Grits Casserole

Servings: 4

Cooking Time: 30 Minutes

Ingredients:

- 10 fresh asparagus spears, cut into 1-inch pieces
- 2 cups cooked grits, cooled to room temperature
- 1 egg, beaten
- 2 teaspoons Worcestershire sauce
- ½ teaspoon garlic powder
- ¼ teaspoon salt
- 2 slices provolone cheese (about 1½ ounces)
- oil for misting or cooking spray

Directions:

1. Mist asparagus spears with oil and cook at 390°F for 5minutes, until crisp-tender.

2. In a medium bowl, mix together the grits, egg, Worcestershire, garlic powder, and salt.

3. Spoon half of grits mixture into air fryer baking pan and top with asparagus.

4. Tear cheese slices into pieces and layer evenly on top of asparagus.

5. Top with remaining grits.

6. Bake at 360°F for 25 minutes. The casserole will rise a little as it cooks. When done, the top will have browned lightly with just a hint of crispiness.

Buttery Rolls

Servings: 6

Cooking Time: 14 Minutes

Ingredients:

- 6½ tablespoons Room-temperature whole or low-fat milk
- 3 tablespoons plus 1 teaspoon Butter, melted and cooled
- 3 tablespoons plus 1 teaspoon (or 1 medium egg, well beaten) Pasteurized egg substitute, such as Egg Beaters
- 1½ tablespoons Granulated white sugar
- 1¼ teaspoons Instant yeast
- ¼ teaspoon Table salt
- 2 cups, plus more for dusting All-purpose flour
- Vegetable oil
- Additional melted butter, for brushing

Directions:

1. Stir the milk, melted butter, pasteurized egg substitute (or whole egg), sugar, yeast, and salt in a medium bowl to combine. Stir in the flour just until the mixture makes a soft dough.

2. Lightly flour a clean, dry work surface. Turn the dough out onto the work surface. Knead the dough for 5 minutes to develop the gluten.

3. Lightly oil the inside of a clean medium bowl. Gather the dough into a compact ball and set it in the bowl. Turn the dough over so that its surface has oil on it all over. Cover the bowl tightly with plastic wrap and set aside in a warm, draft-free place until the dough has doubled in bulk, about 1½ hours.

4. Punch down the dough, then turn it out onto a clean, dry work surface. Divide it into 5 even balls for a small batch, 6 balls for a medium batch, or 8 balls for a large one.

5. For a small batch, lightly oil the inside of a 6-inch round cake pan and set the balls around its perimeter, separating them as much as possible.

6. For a medium batch, lightly oil the inside of a 7-inch round cake pan and set the balls in it with one ball at its center, separating them as much as possible.

7. For a large batch, lightly oil the inside of an 8-inch round cake pan and set the balls in it with one at the center, separating them as much as possible.

8. Cover with plastic wrap and set aside to rise for 30 minutes.

9. Preheat the air fryer to 350°F .

10. Uncover the pan and brush the rolls with a little melted butter, perhaps ½ teaspoon per roll. When the machine is at temperature, set the cake pan in the basket. Air-fry undisturbed for 14 minutes, or until the rolls have risen and browned.

11. Using kitchen tongs and a nonstick-safe spatula, two hot pads, or silicone baking mitts, transfer the cake pan from the basket to a wire rack. Cool the rolls in the pan for a minute or two. Turn the rolls out onto a wire rack, set them top

side up again, and cool for at least another couple of minutes before serving warm.

Okra

Servings: 4
Cooking Time: 12 Minutes

Ingredients:
- 7–8 ounces fresh okra
- 1 egg
- 1 cup milk
- 1 cup breadcrumbs
- ½ teaspoon salt
- oil for misting or cooking spray

Directions:
1. Remove stem ends from okra and cut in ½-inch slices.
2. In a medium bowl, beat together egg and milk. Add okra slices and stir to coat.
3. In a sealable plastic bag or container with lid, mix together the breadcrumbs and salt.
4. Remove okra from egg mixture, letting excess drip off, and transfer into bag with breadcrumbs.
5. Shake okra in crumbs to coat well.
6. Place all of the coated okra into the air fryer basket and mist with oil or cooking spray. Okra doesn't need to cook in a single layer, nor is it necessary to spray all sides at this point. A good spritz on top will do.
7. Cook at 390°F for 5minutes. Shake basket to redistribute and give it another spritz as you shake.
8. Cook 5 more minutes. Shake and spray again. Cook for 2 minutes longer or until golden brown and crispy.

Roasted Corn Salad

Servings: 3
Cooking Time: 15 Minutes

Ingredients:
- 3 4-inch lengths husked and de-silked corn on the cob
- Olive oil spray
- 1 cup Packed baby arugula leaves
- 12 Cherry tomatoes, halved
- Up to 3 Medium scallion(s), trimmed and thinly sliced
- 2 tablespoons Lemon juice
- 1 tablespoon Olive oil
- 1½ teaspoons Honey
- ¼ teaspoon Mild paprika
- ¼ teaspoon Dried oregano
- ¼ teaspoon, plus more to taste Table salt
- ¼ teaspoon Ground black pepper

Directions:
1. Preheat the air fryer to 400°F.
2. When the machine is at temperature, lightly coat the pieces of corn on the cob with olive oil spray. Set the pieces of corn in the basket with as much air space between them as possible. Air-fry undisturbed for 15 minutes, or until the corn is charred in a few spots.
3. Use kitchen tongs to transfer the corn to a wire rack. Cool for 15 minutes.
4. Cut the kernels off the ears by cutting the fat end off each piece so it will stand up straight on a cutting board, then running a knife down the corn. (Or you can save your fingers and buy a fancy tool to remove kernels from corn cobs. Check it out at online kitchenware stores.) Scoop the kernels into a serving bowl.
5. Chop the arugula into bite-size bits and add these to the kernels. Add the tomatoes and scallions, too. Whisk the lemon juice, olive oil, honey, paprika, oregano, salt, and pepper in a small bowl until the honey dissolves. Pour over

the salad and toss well to coat, tasting for extra salt before serving.

Mashed Potato Tots

Servings: 18
Cooking Time: 10 Minutes

Ingredients:
- 1 medium potato or 1 cup cooked mashed potatoes
- 1 tablespoon real bacon bits
- 2 tablespoons chopped green onions, tops only
- ¼ teaspoon onion powder
- 1 teaspoon dried chopped chives
- salt
- 2 tablespoons flour
- 1 egg white, beaten
- ½ cup panko breadcrumbs
- oil for misting or cooking spray

Directions:
1. If using cooked mashed potatoes, jump to step 4.
2. Peel potato and cut into ½-inch cubes. (Small pieces cook more quickly.) Place in saucepan, add water to cover, and heat to boil. Lower heat slightly and continue cooking just until tender, about 10minutes.
3. Drain potatoes and place in ice cold water. Allow to cool for a minute or two, then drain well and mash.
4. Preheat air fryer to 390°F.
5. In a large bowl, mix together the potatoes, bacon bits, onions, onion powder, chives, salt to taste, and flour. Add egg white and stir well.
6. Place panko crumbs on a sheet of wax paper.
7. For each tot, use about 2 teaspoons of potato mixture. To shape, drop the measure of potato mixture onto panko crumbs and push crumbs up and around potatoes to coat edges. Then turn tot over to coat other side with crumbs.
8. Mist tots with oil or cooking spray and place in air fryer basket, crowded but not stacked.
9. Cook at 390°F for 10 minutes, until browned and crispy.
10. Repeat steps 8 and 9 to cook remaining tots.

Roasted Garlic

Servings: 20
Cooking Time: 40 Minutes

Ingredients:
- 20 Peeled medium garlic cloves
- 2 tablespoons, plus more Olive oil

Directions:
1. Preheat the air fryer to 400°F.
2. Set a 10-inch sheet of aluminum foil on your work surface for a small batch, a 14-inch sheet for a medium batch, or a 16-inch sheet for a large batch. Put the garlic cloves in its center in one layer without bunching the cloves together. (Spread them out a little for even cooking.) Drizzle the small batch with 1 tablespoon oil, the medium batch with 2 tablespoons, or the large one with 3 tablespoons. Fold up the sides and seal the foil into a packet.
3. When the machine is at temperature, put the packet in the basket. Air-fry for 40 minutes, or until very fragrant. The cloves inside should be golden and soft.
4. Transfer the packet to a cutting board. Cool for 5 minutes, then open and use the cloves hot. Or cool them to room temperature, set them in a small container or jar, pour in enough olive oil to cover them, seal or cover the container, and refrigerate for up to 2 weeks.

Parmesan Asparagus

Servings: 2

Cooking Time: 5 Minutes

Ingredients:
- 1 bunch asparagus, stems trimmed
- 1 teaspoon olive oil
- salt and freshly ground black pepper
- ¼ cup coarsely grated Parmesan cheese
- ½ lemon

Directions:

1.   Preheat the air fryer to 400°F.

2.   Toss the asparagus with the oil and season with salt and freshly ground black pepper.

3.   Transfer the asparagus to the air fryer basket and air-fry at 400°F for 5 minutes, shaking the basket to turn the asparagus once or twice during the cooking process.

4.   When the asparagus is cooked to your liking, sprinkle the asparagus generously with the Parmesan cheese and close the air fryer drawer again. Let the asparagus sit for 1 minute in the turned-off air fryer. Then, remove the asparagus, transfer it to a serving dish and finish with a grind of black pepper and a squeeze of lemon juice.

Sesame Carrots And Sugar Snap Peas

Servings: 4

Cooking Time: 16 Minutes

Ingredients:
- 1 pound carrots, peeled sliced on the bias (½-inch slices)
- 1 teaspoon olive oil
- salt and freshly ground black pepper
- ⅓ cup honey
- 1 tablespoon sesame oil
- 1 tablespoon soy sauce
- ½ teaspoon minced fresh ginger
- 4 ounces sugar snap peas (about 1 cup)
- 1½ teaspoons sesame seeds

Directions:

1.   Preheat the air fryer to 360°F.

2.   Toss the carrots with the olive oil, season with salt and pepper and air-fry for 10 minutes, shaking the basket once or twice during the cooking process.

3.   Combine the honey, sesame oil, soy sauce and minced ginger in a large bowl. Add the sugar snap peas and the air-fried carrots to the honey mixture, toss to coat and return everything to the air fryer basket.

4.   Turn up the temperature to 400°F and air-fry for an additional 6 minutes, shaking the basket once during the cooking process.

5.   Transfer the carrots and sugar snap peas to a serving bowl. Pour the sauce from the bottom of the cooker over the vegetables and sprinkle sesame seeds over top. Serve immediately.

Panzanella Salad With Crispy Croutons

Servings: 4
Cooking Time: 3 Minutes

Ingredients:

- ½ French baguette, sliced in half lengthwise
- 2 large cloves garlic
- 2 large ripe tomatoes, divided
- 2 small Persian cucumbers, quartered and diced
- ¼ cup Kalamata olives
- 1 tablespoon chopped, fresh oregano or 1 teaspoon dried oregano
- ¼ cup chopped fresh basil
- ¼ cup chopped fresh parsley
- ½ cup sliced red onion
- 2 tablespoons red wine vinegar
- ¼ cup extra-virgin olive oil
- Salt and pepper, to taste

Directions:

1. Preheat the air fryer to 380°F.
2. Place the baguette into the air fryer and toast for 3 to 5 minutes or until lightly golden brown.
3. Remove the bread from air fryer and immediately rub 1 raw garlic clove firmly onto the inside portion of each piece of bread, scraping the garlic onto the bread.
4. Slice 1 of the tomatoes in half and rub the cut edge of one half of the tomato onto the toasted bread. Season the rubbed bread with sea salt to taste.
5. Cut the bread into cubes and place in a large bowl. Cube the remaining 1½ tomatoes and add to the bowl. Add the cucumbers, olives, oregano, basil, parsley, and onion; stir to mix. Drizzle the red wine vinegar into the bowl, and stir. Drizzle the olive oil over the top, stir, and adjust the seasonings with salt and pepper.
6. Serve immediately or allow to sit at room temperature up to 1 hour before serving.

Salt And Pepper Baked Potatoes

Servings: 4
Cooking Time: 40 Minutes

Ingredients:

- 1 to 2 tablespoons olive oil
- 4 medium russet potatoes (about 9 to 10 ounces each)
- salt and coarsely ground black pepper
- butter, sour cream, chopped fresh chives, scallions or bacon bits (optional)

Directions:

1. Preheat the air fryer to 400°F.
2. Rub the olive oil all over the potatoes and season them generously with salt and coarsely ground black pepper. Pierce all sides of the potatoes several times with the tines of a fork.
3. Air-fry for 40 minutes, turning the potatoes over halfway through the cooking time.
4. Serve the potatoes, split open with butter, sour cream, fresh chives, scallions or bacon bits.

Five-spice Roasted Sweet Potatoes

Servings: 4
Cooking Time: 12 Minutes

Ingredients:

- ½ teaspoon ground cinnamon
- ¼ teaspoon ground cumin
- ¼ teaspoon paprika
- 1 teaspoon chile powder
- ⅛ teaspoon turmeric
- ½ teaspoon salt (optional)
- freshly ground black pepper

- 2 large sweet potatoes, peeled and cut into ¾-inch cubes (about 3 cups)
- 1 tablespoon olive oil

Directions:

1. In a large bowl, mix together cinnamon, cumin, paprika, chile powder, turmeric, salt, and pepper to taste.
2. Add potatoes and stir well.
3. Drizzle the seasoned potatoes with the olive oil and stir until evenly coated.
4. Place seasoned potatoes in the air fryer baking pan or an ovenproof dish that fits inside your air fryer basket.
5. Cook for 6minutes at 390°F, stop, and stir well.
6. Cook for an additional 6minutes.

Fried Eggplant Balls

Servings: 4

Cooking Time: 40 Minutes

Ingredients:
- 1 medium eggplant (about 1 pound)
- olive oil
- salt and freshly ground black pepper
- 1 cup grated Parmesan cheese
- 2 cups fresh breadcrumbs
- 2 tablespoons chopped fresh parsley
- 2 tablespoons chopped fresh basil
- 1 clove garlic, minced
- 1 egg, lightly beaten
- ½ cup fine dried breadcrumbs

Directions:

1. Preheat the air fryer to 400°F.
2. Quarter the eggplant by cutting it in half both lengthwise and horizontally. Make a few slashes in the flesh of the eggplant but not through the skin. Brush the cut surface of the eggplant generously with olive oil and transfer to the air fryer basket, cut side up. Air-fry for 10 minutes. Turn the eggplant quarters cut side down and air-fry for another 15 minutes or until the eggplant is soft all the way through. You may need to rotate the pieces in the air fryer so that they cook evenly. Transfer the eggplant to a cutting board to cool.
3. Place the Parmesan cheese, the fresh breadcrumbs, fresh herbs, garlic and egg in a food processor. Scoop the flesh out of the eggplant, discarding the skin and any pieces that are tough. You should have about 1 to 1½ cups of eggplant. Add the eggplant to the food processor and process everything together until smooth. Season with salt and pepper. Refrigerate the mixture for at least 30 minutes.
4. Place the dried breadcrumbs into a shallow dish or onto a plate. Scoop heaping tablespoons of the eggplant mixture into the dried breadcrumbs. Roll the dollops of eggplant in the breadcrumbs and then shape into small balls. You should have 16 to 18 eggplant balls at the end. Refrigerate until you are ready to air-fry.
5. Preheat the air fryer to 350°F.
6. Spray the eggplant balls and the air fryer basket with olive oil. Air-fry the eggplant balls for 15 minutes, rotating the balls during the cooking process to brown evenly.

Pork Tenderloin Salad

Servings: 4

Cooking Time: 25 Minutes

Ingredients:

- Pork Tenderloin
- ½ teaspoon smoked paprika
- ¼ teaspoon salt
- ¼ teaspoon garlic powder
- ½ teaspoon onion powder
- ⅛ teaspoon ginger
- 1 teaspoon extra-light olive oil
- ¾ pound pork tenderloin
- Dressing
- 3 tablespoons extra-light olive oil
- 2 tablespoons red wine vinegar
- 2 tablespoons Dijon mustard
- 1 tablespoon honey
- Salad
- ¼ sweet red bell pepper
- 1 large Granny Smith apple
- 8 cups shredded Napa cabbage

Directions:

1. Mix the tenderloin seasonings together with oil and rub all over surface of meat.

2. Place pork tenderloin in the air fryer basket and cook at 390°F for 25minutes, until meat registers 130°F on a meat thermometer.

3. Allow meat to rest while preparing salad and dressing.

4. In a jar, shake all dressing ingredients together until well mixed.

5. Cut the bell pepper into slivers, then core, quarter, and slice the apple crosswise.

6. In a large bowl, toss together the cabbage, bell pepper, apple, and dressing.

7. Divide salad mixture among 4 plates.

8. Slice pork tenderloin into ½-inch slices and divide among the 4 salads.

9. Serve with sweet potato or other vegetable chips.

Rosemary Roasted Potatoes With Lemon

Servings: 4

Cooking Time: 12 Minutes

Ingredients:

- 1 pound small red-skinned potatoes, halved or cut into bite-sized chunks
- 1 tablespoon olive oil
- 1 teaspoon finely chopped fresh rosemary
- ¼ teaspoon salt
- freshly ground black pepper
- 1 tablespoon lemon zest

Directions:

1. Preheat the air fryer to 400°F.

2. Toss the potatoes with the olive oil, rosemary, salt and freshly ground black pepper.

3. Air-fry for 12 minutes (depending on the size of the chunks), tossing the potatoes a few times throughout the cooking process.

4. As soon as the potatoes are tender to a knifepoint, toss them with the lemon zest and more salt if desired.

Wilted Brussels Sprout Slaw

Servings: 4

Cooking Time: 18 Minutes

Ingredients:

- 2 Thick-cut bacon strip(s), halved widthwise (gluten-free, if a concern)
- 4½ cups (about 1 pound 2 ounces) Bagged shredded Brussels sprouts

- ¼ teaspoon Table salt
- 2 tablespoons White balsamic vinegar (see here)
- 2 teaspoons Worcestershire sauce (gluten-free, if a concern)
- 1 teaspoon Dijon mustard (gluten-free, if a concern)
- ¼ teaspoon Ground black pepper

Directions:

1. Preheat the air fryer to 375°F .
2. When the machine is at temperature, lay the bacon strip halves in the basket in one layer and air-fry for 10 minutes, or until crisp.
3. Use kitchen tongs to transfer the bacon pieces to a wire rack. Put the shredded Brussels sprouts in a large bowl. Drain any fat from the basket or the tray under the basket onto the Brussels sprouts. Add the salt and toss well to coat.
4. Put the Brussels sprout shreds in the basket, spreading them out into as close to an even layer as you can. Air-fry for 8 minutes, tossing the basket's contents at least three times, until wilted and lightly browned.
5. Pour the contents of the basket into a serving bowl. Chop the bacon and add it to the Brussels sprouts. Add the vinegar, Worcestershire sauce, mustard, and pepper. Toss well to blend the dressing and coat the Brussels sprout shreds. Serve warm.

Cauliflower

Servings: 4
Cooking Time: 6 Minutes

Ingredients:

- ½ cup water
- 1 10-ounce package frozen cauliflower (florets)
- 1 teaspoon lemon pepper seasoning

Directions:

1. Pour the water into air fryer drawer.
2. Pour the frozen cauliflower into the air fryer basket and sprinkle with lemon pepper seasoning.
3. Cook at 390°F for approximately 6 minutes.

Buttery Stuffed Tomatoes

Servings: 6
Cooking Time: 15 Minutes

Ingredients:

- 3 8-ounce round tomatoes
- ½ cup plus 1 tablespoon Plain panko bread crumbs (gluten-free, if a concern)
- 3 tablespoons (about ½ ounce) Finely grated Parmesan cheese
- 3 tablespoons Butter, melted and cooled
- 4 teaspoons Stemmed and chopped fresh parsley leaves
- 1 teaspoon Minced garlic
- ¼ teaspoon Table salt
- Up to ¼ teaspoon Red pepper flakes
- Olive oil spray

Directions:

1. Preheat the air fryer to 375°F .
2. Cut the tomatoes in half through their "equators" (that is, not through the stem ends). One at a time, gently squeeze the tomato halves over a trash can, using a clean finger to gently force out the seeds and most of the juice inside, working carefully so that the tomato doesn't lose its round shape or get crushed.
3. Stir the bread crumbs, cheese, butter, parsley, garlic, salt, and red pepper flakes in a bowl until the bread crumbs are moistened and the parsley is uniform throughout the mixture. Pile this mixture into the spaces left in the tomato halves.

Press gently to compact the filling. Coat the tops of the tomatoes with olive oil spray.

4. Place the tomatoes cut side up in the basket. They may touch each other. Air-fry for 15 minutes, or until the filling is lightly browned and crunchy.

5. Use nonstick-safe spatula and kitchen tongs for balance to gently transfer the stuffed tomatoes to a platter or a cutting board. Cool for a couple of minutes before serving.

Fried Okra

Servings: 4
Cooking Time: 8 Minutes

Ingredients:
- 1 pound okra
- 1 large egg
- 1 tablespoon milk
- 1 teaspoon salt, divided
- ½ teaspoon black pepper, divided
- ¼ teaspoon paprika
- ¼ teaspoon thyme
- ½ cup cornmeal
- ½ cup all-purpose flour

Directions:
1. Preheat the air fryer to 400°F.
2. Cut the okra into ½-inch rounds.
3. In a medium bowl, whisk together the egg, milk, ½ teaspoon of the salt, and ¼ teaspoon of black pepper. Place the okra into the egg mixture and toss until well coated.
4. In a separate bowl, mix together the remaining ½ teaspoon of salt, the remaining ¼ teaspoon of black pepper, the paprika, the thyme, the cornmeal, and the flour. Working in small batches, dredge the egg-coated okra in the cornmeal mixture until all the okra has been breaded.

5. Place a single layer of okra in the air fryer basket and spray with cooking spray. Cook for 4 minutes, toss to check for crispness, and cook another 4 minutes. Repeat in batches, as needed.

Cheesy Texas Toast

Servings: 2
Cooking Time: 4 Minutes

Ingredients:
- 2 1-inch-thick slice(s) Italian bread (each about 4 inches across)
- 4 teaspoons Softened butter
- 2 teaspoons Minced garlic
- ¼ cup (about ¾ ounce) Finely grated Parmesan cheese

Directions:
1. Preheat the air fryer to 400°F.
2. Spread one side of a slice of bread with 2 teaspoons butter. Sprinkle with 1 teaspoon minced garlic, followed by 2 tablespoons grated cheese. Repeat this process if you're making one or more additional toasts.
3. When the machine is at temperature, put the bread slice(s) cheese side up in the basket (with as much air space between them as possible if you're making more than one). Air-fry undisturbed for 4 minutes, or until browned and crunchy.
4. Use a nonstick-safe spatula to transfer the toasts cheese side up to a wire rack. Cool for 5 minutes before serving.

Salmon Salad With Steamboat Dressing

Servings: 4
Cooking Time: 18 Minutes

Ingredients:
- ¼ teaspoon salt
- 1½ teaspoons dried dill weed
- 1 tablespoon fresh lemon juice
- 8 ounces fresh or frozen salmon fillet (skin on)
- 8 cups shredded romaine, Boston, or other leaf lettuce
- 8 spears cooked asparagus, cut in 1-inch pieces
- 8 cherry tomatoes, halved or quartered

Directions:

1. Mix the salt and dill weed together. Rub the lemon juice over the salmon on both sides and sprinkle the dill and salt all over. Refrigerate for 15 to 20minutes.

2. Make Steamboat Dressing and refrigerate while cooking salmon and preparing salad.

3. Cook salmon in air fryer basket at 330°F for 18 minutes. Cooking time will vary depending on thickness of fillets. When done, salmon should flake with fork but still be moist and tender.

4. Remove salmon from air fryer and cool slightly. At this point, the skin should slide off easily. Cut salmon into 4 pieces and discard skin.

5. Divide the lettuce among 4 plates. Scatter asparagus spears and tomato pieces evenly over the lettuce, allowing roughly 2 whole spears and 2 whole cherry tomatoes per plate.

6. Top each salad with one portion of the salmon and drizzle with a tablespoon of dressing. Serve with additional dressing to pass at the table.

Beef，pork & Lamb Recipes

Calf's Liver

Servings: 4
Cooking Time: 5 Minutes

Ingredients:

- 1 pound sliced calf's liver
- salt and pepper
- 2 eggs
- 2 tablespoons milk
- ½ cup whole wheat flour
- 1½ cups panko breadcrumbs
- ½ cup plain breadcrumbs
- ½ teaspoon salt
- ¼ teaspoon pepper
- oil for misting or cooking spray

Directions:

1. Cut liver slices crosswise into strips about ½-inch wide. Sprinkle with salt and pepper to taste.
2. Beat together egg and milk in a shallow dish.
3. Place wheat flour in a second shallow dish.
4. In a third shallow dish, mix together panko, plain breadcrumbs, ½ teaspoon salt, and ¼ teaspoon pepper.
5. Preheat air fryer to 390°F.
6. Dip liver strips in flour, egg wash, and then breadcrumbs, pressing in coating slightly to make crumbs stick.
7. Cooking half the liver at a time, place strips in air fryer basket in a single layer, close but not touching. Cook at 390°F for 5 minutes or until done to your preference.
8. Repeat step 7 to cook remaining liver.

Apple Cornbread Stuffed Pork Loin With Apple Gravy

Servings: 4
Cooking Time: 61 Minutes

Ingredients:

- 4 strips of bacon, chopped
- 1 Granny Smith apple, peeled, cored and finely chopped
- 2 teaspoons fresh thyme leaves
- ¼ cup chopped fresh parsley
- 2 cups cubed cornbread
- ½ cup chicken stock
- salt and freshly ground black pepper
- 1 (2-pound) boneless pork loin
- kitchen twine
- Apple Gravy:
- 2 tablespoons butter
- 1 shallot, minced
- 1 Granny Smith apple, peeled, cored and finely chopped
- 3 sprigs fresh thyme
- 2 tablespoons flour
- 1 cup chicken stock
- ½ cup apple cider
- salt and freshly ground black pepper, to taste

Directions:

1. Preheat the air fryer to 400°F.
2. Add the bacon to the air fryer and air-fry for 6 minutes until crispy. While the bacon is cooking, combine the apple, fresh thyme, parsley and cornbread in a bowl and toss well. Moisten the mixture with the chicken stock and season to taste with salt and freshly ground black pepper. Add the cooked bacon to the mixture.

3. Butterfly the pork loin by holding it flat on the cutting board with one hand, while slicing into the pork loin parallel to the cutting board with the other. Slice into the longest side of the pork loin, but stop before you cut all the way through. You should then be able to open the pork loin up like a book, making it twice as wide as it was when you started. Season the inside of the pork with salt and freshly ground black pepper.

4. Spread the cornbread mixture onto the butterflied pork loin, leaving a one-inch border around the edge of the pork. Roll the pork loin up around the stuffing to enclose the stuffing, and tie the rolled pork in several places with kitchen twine or secure with toothpicks. Try to replace any stuffing that falls out of the roast as you roll it, by stuffing it into the ends of the rolled pork. Season the outside of the pork with salt and freshly ground black pepper.

5. Preheat the air fryer to 360°F.

6. Place the stuffed pork loin into the air fryer, seam side down. Air-fry the pork loin for 15 minutes at 360°F. Turn the pork loin over and air-fry for an additional 15 minutes. Turn the pork loin a quarter turn and air-fry for an additional 15 minutes. Turn the pork loin over again to expose the fourth side, and air-fry for an additional 10 minutes. The pork loin should register 155°F on an instant read thermometer when it is finished.

7. While the pork is cooking, make the apple gravy. Preheat a saucepan over medium heat on the stovetop and melt the butter. Add the shallot, apple and thyme sprigs and sauté until the apple starts to soften and brown a little. Add the flour and stir for a minute or two. Whisk in the stock and apple cider vigorously to prevent the flour from forming lumps. Bring the mixture to a boil to thicken and season to taste with salt and pepper.

8. Transfer the pork loin to a resting plate and loosely tent with foil, letting the pork rest for at least 5 minutes before slicing and serving with the apple gravy poured over the top.

Pretzel-coated Pork Tenderloin

Servings: 4

Cooking Time: 10 Minutes

Ingredients:

- 1 Large egg white(s)
- 2 teaspoons Dijon mustard (gluten-free, if a concern)
- 1½ cups (about 6 ounces) Crushed pretzel crumbs (see the headnote; gluten-free, if a concern)
- 1 pound (4 sections) Pork tenderloin, cut into ¼-pound (4-ounce) sections
- Vegetable oil spray

Directions:

1. Preheat the air fryer to 350°F .

2. Set up and fill two shallow soup plates or small pie plates on your counter: one for the egg white(s), whisked with the mustard until foamy; and one for the pretzel crumbs.

3. Dip a section of pork tenderloin in the egg white mixture and turn it to coat well, even on the ends. Let any excess egg white mixture slip back into the rest, then set the pork in the pretzel crumbs. Roll it several times, pressing gently, until the pork is evenly coated, even on the ends. Generously coat the pork section with vegetable oil spray, set it aside, and continue coating and spraying the remaining sections.

4. Set the pork sections in the basket with at least ¼ inch between them. Air-fry undisturbed for 10 minutes, or until an instant-read meat thermometer inserted into the center of one section registers 145°F.

5. Use kitchen tongs to transfer the pieces to a wire rack. Cool for 3 to 5 minutes before serving.

Carne Asada

Servings: 4
Cooking Time: 15 Minutes

Ingredients:
- 4 cloves garlic, minced
- 3 chipotle peppers in adobo, chopped
- ⅓ cup chopped fresh parsley
- ⅓ cup chopped fresh oregano
- 1 teaspoon ground cumin seed
- juice of 2 limes
- ⅓ cup olive oil
- 1 to 1½ pounds flank steak (depending on your appetites)
- salt
- tortillas and guacamole (optional – for serving)

Directions:
1. Make the marinade: Combine the garlic, chipotle, parsley, oregano, cumin, lime juice and olive oil in a non-reactive bowl. Coat the flank steak with the marinade and let it marinate for 30 minutes to 8 hours. (Don't leave the steak out of refrigeration for longer than 2 hours, however.)
2. Preheat the air fryer to 390°F.
3. Remove the steak from the marinade and place it in the air fryer basket. Season the steak with salt and air-fry for 15 minutes, turning the steak over halfway through the cooking time and seasoning again with salt. This should cook the

steak to medium. Add or subtract two minutes for medium-well or medium-rare.
4. Remember to let the steak rest before slicing the meat against the grain. Serve with warm tortillas, guacamole and a fresh salsa like the Tomato-Corn Salsa below.

Red Curry Flank Steak

Servings: 4
Cooking Time: 18 Minutes

Ingredients:
- 3 tablespoons red curry paste
- ¼ cup olive oil
- 2 teaspoons grated fresh ginger
- 2 tablespoons soy sauce
- 2 tablespoons rice wine vinegar
- 3 scallions, minced
- 1½ pounds flank steak
- fresh cilantro (or parsley) leaves

Directions:
1. Mix the red curry paste, olive oil, ginger, soy sauce, rice vinegar and scallions together in a bowl. Place the flank steak in a shallow glass dish and pour half the marinade over the steak. Pierce the steak several times with a fork or meat tenderizer to let the marinade penetrate the meat. Turn the steak over, pour the remaining marinade over the top and pierce the steak several times again. Cover and marinate the steak in the refrigerator for 6 to 8 hours.
2. When you are ready to cook, remove the steak from the refrigerator and let it sit at room temperature for 30 minutes.
3. Preheat the air fryer to 400°F.
4. Cut the flank steak in half so that it fits more easily into the air fryer and transfer both pieces to the air fryer basket. Pour the marinade over the

steak. Air-fry for 18 minutes, depending on your preferred degree of doneness of the steak (12 minutes = medium rare). Flip the steak over halfway through the cooking time.

5. When your desired degree of doneness has been reached, remove the steak to a cutting board and let it rest for 5 minutes before slicing. Thinly slice the flank steak against the grain of the meat. Transfer the slices to a serving platter, pour any juice from the bottom of the air fryer over the sliced flank steak and sprinkle the fresh cilantro on top.

Pork Chops

Servings: 2
Cooking Time: 16 Minutes

Ingredients:
- 2 bone-in, centercut pork chops, 1-inch thick (10 ounces each)
- 2 teaspoons Worcestershire sauce
- salt and pepper
- cooking spray

Directions:
1. Rub the Worcestershire sauce into both sides of pork chops.
2. Season with salt and pepper to taste.
3. Spray air fryer basket with cooking spray and place the chops in basket side by side.
4. Cook at 360°F for 16 minutes or until well done. Let rest for 5minutes before serving.

Teriyaki Country-style Pork Ribs

Servings: 3
Cooking Time: 30 Minutes

Ingredients:
- 3 tablespoons Regular or low-sodium soy sauce or gluten-free tamari sauce
- 3 tablespoons Honey
- ¾ teaspoon Ground dried ginger
- ¾ teaspoon Garlic powder
- 3 8-ounce boneless country-style pork ribs
- Vegetable oil spray

Directions:
1. Preheat the air fryer to 350°F .
2. Mix the soy or tamari sauce, honey, ground ginger, and garlic powder in another bowl until uniform.
3. Smear about half of this teriyaki sauce over all sides of the country-style ribs. Reserve the remainder of the teriyaki sauce. Generously coat the meat with vegetable oil spray.
4. When the machine is at temperature, place the country-style ribs in the basket with as much air space between them as possible. Air-fry undisturbed for 15 minutes. Turn the country-style ribs (but keep the space between them) and brush them all over with the remaining teriyaki sauce. Continue air-frying undisturbed for 15 minutes, or until an instant-read meat thermometer inserted into the center of one rib registers at least 145°F.
5. Use kitchen tongs to transfer the country-style ribs to a wire rack. Cool for 5 minutes before serving.

Kielbasa Sausage With Pierogies And Caramelized Onions

Servings: 3
Cooking Time: 30 Minutes

Ingredients:
- 1 Vidalia or sweet onion, sliced
- olive oil
- salt and freshly ground black pepper
- 2 tablespoons butter, cut into small cubes

- 1 teaspoon sugar
- 1 pound light Polish kielbasa sausage, cut into 2-inch chunks
- 1 (13-ounce) package frozen mini pierogies
- 2 teaspoons vegetable or olive oil
- chopped scallions

Directions:

1. Preheat the air fryer to 400°F.

2. Toss the sliced onions with a little olive oil, salt and pepper and transfer them to the air fryer basket. Dot the onions with pieces of butter and air-fry at 400°F for 2 minutes. Then sprinkle the sugar over the onions and stir. Pour any melted butter from the bottom of the air fryer drawer over the onions (do this over the sink – some of the butter will spill through the basket). Continue to air-fry for another 13 minutes, stirring or shaking the basket every few minutes to cook the onions evenly.

3. Add the kielbasa chunks to the onions and toss. Air-fry for another 5 minutes, shaking the basket halfway through the cooking time. Transfer the kielbasa and onions to a bowl and cover with aluminum foil to keep warm.

4. Toss the frozen pierogies with the vegetable or olive oil and transfer them to the air fryer basket. Air-fry at 400°F for 8 minutes, shaking the basket twice during the cooking time.

5. When the pierogies have finished cooking, return the kielbasa and onions to the air fryer and gently toss with the pierogies. Air-fry for 2 more minutes and then transfer everything to a serving platter. Garnish with the chopped scallions and serve hot with the spicy sour cream sauce below.

6. Kielbasa Sausage with Pierogies and Caramelized Onions

Pork & Beef Egg Rolls

Servings: 8
Cooking Time: 8 Minutes

Ingredients:

- ¼ pound very lean ground beef
- ¼ pound lean ground pork
- 1 tablespoon soy sauce
- 1 teaspoon olive oil
- ½ cup grated carrots
- 2 green onions, chopped
- 2 cups grated Napa cabbage
- ¼ cup chopped water chestnuts
- ¼ teaspoon salt
- ¼ teaspoon garlic powder
- ¼ teaspoon black pepper
- 1 egg
- 1 tablespoon water
- 8 egg roll wraps
- oil for misting or cooking spray

Directions:

1. In a large skillet, brown beef and pork with soy sauce. Remove cooked meat from skillet, drain, and set aside.

2. Pour off any excess grease from skillet. Add olive oil, carrots, and onions. Sauté until barely tender, about 1 minute.

3. Stir in cabbage, cover, and cook for 1 minute or just until cabbage slightly wilts. Remove from heat.

4. In a large bowl, combine the cooked meats and vegetables, water chestnuts, salt, garlic powder, and pepper. Stir well. If needed, add more salt to taste.

5. Beat together egg and water in a small bowl.

6. Fill egg roll wrappers, using about ¼ cup of filling for each wrap. Roll up and brush all over

with egg wash to seal. Spray very lightly with olive oil or cooking spray.

7. Place 4 egg rolls in air fryer basket and cook at 390°F for 4minutes. Turn over and cook 4 more minutes, until golden brown and crispy.

8. Repeat to cook remaining egg rolls.

Meatloaf With Tangy Tomato Glaze

Servings: 6
Cooking Time: 50 Minutes

Ingredients:

- 1 pound ground beef
- ½ pound ground pork
- ½ pound ground veal (or turkey)
- 1 medium onion, diced
- 1 small clove of garlic, minced
- 2 egg yolks, lightly beaten
- ½ cup tomato ketchup
- 1 tablespoon Worcestershire sauce
- ½ cup plain breadcrumbs*
- 2 teaspoons salt
- freshly ground black pepper
- ½ cup chopped fresh parsley, plus more for garnish
- 6 tablespoons ketchup
- 1 tablespoon balsamic vinegar
- 2 tablespoons brown sugar

Directions:

1. Combine the meats, onion, garlic, egg yolks, ketchup, Worcestershire sauce, breadcrumbs, salt, pepper and fresh parsley in a large bowl and mix well.

2. Preheat the air fryer to 350°F and pour a little water into the bottom of the air fryer drawer. (This will help prevent the grease that drips into the bottom drawer from burning and smoking.)

3. Transfer the meatloaf mixture to the air fryer basket, packing it down gently. Run a spatula around the meatloaf to create a space about ½-inch wide between the meat and the side of the air fryer basket.

4. Air-fry at 350°F for 20 minutes. Carefully invert the meatloaf onto a plate (remember to remove the basket from the air fryer drawer so you don't pour all the grease out) and slide it back into the air fryer basket to turn it over. Re-shape the meatloaf with a spatula if necessary. Air-fry for another 20 minutes at 350°F.

5. Combine the ketchup, balsamic vinegar and brown sugar in a bowl and spread the mixture over the meatloaf. Air-fry for another 10 minutes, until an instant read thermometer inserted into the center of the meatloaf registers 160°F.

6. Allow the meatloaf to rest for a few more minutes and then transfer it to a serving platter using a spatula. Slice the meatloaf, sprinkle a little chopped parsley on top if desired, and serve.

Pepper Steak

Servings: 4
Cooking Time: 30 Minutes

Ingredients:

- 2 tablespoons cornstarch
- 1 tablespoon sugar
- ¾ cup beef broth
- ¼ cup hoisin sauce
- 3 tablespoons soy sauce
- 1 teaspoon sesame oil
- ½ teaspoon freshly ground black pepper
- 1½ pounds boneless New York strip steaks, sliced into ½-inch strips
- 1 onion, sliced

- 3 small bell peppers, red, yellow and green, sliced

Directions:

1. Whisk the cornstarch and sugar together in a large bowl to break up any lumps in the cornstarch. Add the beef broth and whisk until combined and smooth. Stir in the hoisin sauce, soy sauce, sesame oil and freshly ground black pepper. Add the beef, onion and peppers, and toss to coat. Marinate the beef and vegetables at room temperature for 30 minutes, stirring a few times to keep meat and vegetables coated.

2. Preheat the air fryer to 350°F.

3. Transfer the beef, onion, and peppers to the air fryer basket with tongs, reserving the marinade. Air-fry the beef and vegetables for 30 minutes, stirring well two or three times during the cooking process.

4. While the beef is air-frying, bring the reserved marinade to a simmer in a small saucepan over medium heat on the stovetop. Simmer for 5 minutes until the sauce thickens.

5. When the steak and vegetables have finished cooking, transfer them to a serving platter. Pour the hot sauce over the pepper steak and serve with white rice.

Chicken-fried Steak

Servings: 2
Cooking Time: 12 Minutes

Ingredients:

- 1½ cups All-purpose flour
- 2 Large egg(s)
- 2 tablespoons Regular or low-fat sour cream
- 2 tablespoons Worcestershire sauce
- 2 ¼-pound thin beef cube steak(s)
- Vegetable oil spray

Directions:

1. Preheat the air fryer to 400°F.

2. Set up and fill two shallow soup plates or small pie plates on your counter: one for the flour; and one for the egg(s), whisked with the sour cream and Worcestershire sauce until uniform.

3. Dredge a piece of beef in the flour, coating it well on both sides and even along the edge. Shake off any excess; then dip the meat in the egg mixture, coating both sides while retaining the flour on the meat. Let any excess egg mixture slip back into the rest. Dredge the meat in the flour once again, coating all surfaces well. Gently shake off the excess coating and set the steak aside if you're coating another steak or two. Once done, coat the steak(s) on both sides with the vegetable oil spray.

4. Set the steak(s) in the basket. If there's more than one steak, make sure they do not overlap or even touch, although the smallest gap between them is enough to get them crunchy. Air-fry undisturbed for 6 minutes.

5. Use kitchen tongs to pick up one of the steaks. Coat it again on both sides with vegetable oil spray. Turn it upside down and set it back in the basket with that same regard for the space between them in larger batches. Repeat with any other steaks. Continue air-frying undisturbed for 6 minutes, or until golden brown and crunchy.

6. Use kitchen tongs to transfer the steak(s) to a wire rack. Cool for 5 minutes before serving.

Steakhouse Burgers With Red Onion Compote

Servings: 4

Cooking Time: 22 Minutes

Ingredients:

- 1½ pounds lean ground beef
- 2 cloves garlic, minced and divided
- 1 teaspoon Worcestershire sauce
- 1 teaspoon sea salt, divided
- ½ teaspoon black pepper
- 1 tablespoon extra-virgin olive oil
- 1 red onion, thinly sliced
- ¼ cup balsamic vinegar
- 1 teaspoon sugar
- 1 tablespoon tomato paste
- 2 tablespoons mayonnaise
- 2 tablespoons sour cream
- 4 brioche hamburger buns
- 1 cup arugula

Directions:

1. In a large bowl, mix together the ground beef, 1 of the minced garlic cloves, the Worcestershire sauce, ½ teaspoon of the salt, and the black pepper. Form the meat into 1-inch-thick patties. Make a dent in the center (this helps the center cook evenly). Let the meat sit for 15 minutes.

2. Meanwhile, in a small saucepan over medium heat, cook the olive oil and red onion for 4 minutes, stirring frequently to avoid burning. Add in the balsamic vinegar, sugar, and tomato paste, and cook for an additional 3 minutes, stirring frequently. Transfer the onion compote to a small bowl.

3. Preheat the air fryer to 350°F.

4. In another small bowl, mix together the remaining minced garlic, the mayonnaise, and the sour cream. Spread the mayo mixture on the insides of the brioche buns.

5. Cook the hamburgers for 6 minutes, flip the burgers, and cook an additional 2 to 6 minutes. Check the internal temperature to avoid under- or overcooking. Hamburgers should be cooked to at least 160°F. After cooking, cover with foil and let the meat rest for 5 minutes.

6. Meanwhile, place the buns inside the air fryer and toast them for 3 minutes.

7. To assemble the burgers, place the hamburger on one side of the bun, top with onion compote and ¼ cup arugula, and then place the other half of the bun on top.

Natchitoches Meat Pies

Servings: 8

Cooking Time: 12 Minutes

Ingredients:

- Filling
- ½ pound lean ground beef
- ¼ cup finely chopped onion
- ¼ cup finely chopped green bell pepper
- ⅛ teaspoon salt
- ½ teaspoon garlic powder
- ½ teaspoon red pepper flakes
- 1 tablespoon low sodium Worcestershire sauce
- Crust
- 2 cups self-rising flour
- ¼ cup butter, finely diced
- 1 cup milk
- Egg Wash
- 1 egg
- 1 tablespoon water or milk
- oil for misting or cooking spray

Directions:

1. Mix all filling ingredients well and shape into 4 small patties.

2. Cook patties in air fryer basket at 390°F for 10 to 12minutes or until well done.

3. Place patties in large bowl and use fork and knife to crumble meat into very small pieces. Set aside.

4. To make the crust, use a pastry blender or fork to cut the butter into the flour until well mixed. Add milk and stir until dough stiffens.

5. Divide dough into 8 equal portions.

6. On a lightly floured surface, roll each portion of dough into a circle. The circle should be thin and about 5 inches in diameter, but don't worry about getting a perfect shape. Uneven circles result in a rustic look that many people prefer.

7. Spoon 2 tablespoons of meat filling onto each dough circle.

8. Brush egg wash all the way around the edge of dough circle, about ½-inch deep.

9. Fold each circle in half and press dough with tines of a dinner fork to seal the edges all the way around.

10. Brush tops of sealed meat pies with egg wash.

11. Cook filled pies in a single layer in air fryer basket at 360°F for 4minutes. Spray tops with oil or cooking spray, turn pies over, and spray bottoms with oil or cooking spray. Cook for an additional 2minutes.

12. Repeat previous step to cook remaining pies.

Rack Of Lamb With Pistachio Crust

Servings: 2

Cooking Time: 19 Minutes

Ingredients:

- ½ cup finely chopped pistachios
- 3 tablespoons panko breadcrumbs
- 1 teaspoon chopped fresh rosemary
- 2 teaspoons chopped fresh oregano
- salt and freshly ground black pepper
- 1 tablespoon olive oil
- 1 rack of lamb, bones trimmed of fat and frenched
- 1 tablespoon Dijon mustard

Directions:

1. Preheat the air fryer to 380°F.

2. Combine the pistachios, breadcrumbs, rosemary, oregano, salt and pepper in a small bowl. Drizzle in the olive oil and stir to combine.

3. Season the rack of lamb with salt and pepper on all sides and transfer it to the air fryer basket with the fat side facing up. Air-fry the lamb for 12 minutes. Remove the lamb from the air fryer and brush the fat side of the lamb rack with the Dijon mustard. Coat the rack with the pistachio mixture, pressing the breadcrumbs onto the lamb with your hands and rolling the bottom of the rack in any of the crumbs that fall off.

4. Return the rack of lamb to the air fryer and air-fry for another 3 to 7 minutes or until an instant read thermometer reads 140°F for medium. Add or subtract a couple of minutes for lamb that is more or less well cooked. (Your time will vary depending on how big the rack of lamb is.)

5. Let the lamb rest for at least 5 minutes. Then, slice into chops and serve.

Bacon, Blue Cheese And Pear Stuffed Pork Chops

Servings: 3
Cooking Time: 24 Minutes

Ingredients:

- 4 slices bacon, chopped
- 1 tablespoon butter
- ½ cup finely diced onion
- ⅓ cup chicken stock
- 1½ cups seasoned stuffing cubes
- 1 egg, beaten
- ½ teaspoon dried thyme
- ½ teaspoon salt
- ⅛ teaspoon black pepper
- 1 pear, finely diced
- ⅓ cup crumbled blue cheese
- 3 boneless center-cut pork chops (2-inch thick)
- olive oil
- salt and freshly ground black pepper

Directions:

1. Preheat the air fryer to 400°F.
2. Place the bacon into the air fryer basket and air-fry for 6 minutes, stirring halfway through the cooking time. Remove the bacon and set it aside on a paper towel. Pour out the grease from the bottom of the air fryer.
3. To make the stuffing, melt the butter in a medium saucepan over medium heat on the stovetop. Add the onion and sauté for a few minutes, until it starts to soften. Add the chicken stock and simmer for 1 minute. Remove the pan from the heat and add the stuffing cubes. Stir until the stock has been absorbed. Add the egg, dried thyme, salt and freshly ground black pepper, and stir until combined. Fold in the diced pear and crumbled blue cheese.
4. Place the pork chops on a cutting board. Using the palm of your hand to hold the chop flat and steady, slice into the side of the pork chop to make a pocket in the center of the chop. Leave about an inch of chop uncut and make sure you don't cut all the way through the pork chop. Brush both sides of the pork chops with olive oil and season with salt and freshly ground black pepper. Stuff each pork chop with a third of the stuffing, packing the stuffing tightly inside the pocket.
5. Preheat the air fryer to 360°F.
6. Spray or brush the sides of the air fryer basket with oil. Place the pork chops in the air fryer basket with the open stuffed edge of the pork chop facing the outside edges of the basket.
7. Air-fry the pork chops for 18 minutes, turning the pork chops over halfway through the cooking time. When the chops are done, let them rest for 5 minutes and then transfer to a serving platter.

Zesty London Broil

Servings: 4
Cooking Time: 28 Minutes

Ingredients:

- ⅔ cup ketchup
- ¼ cup honey
- ¼ cup olive oil
- 2 tablespoons apple cider vinegar
- 2 tablespoons Worcestershire sauce
- 2 tablespoons minced onion
- ½ teaspoon paprika
- 1 teaspoon salt
- 1 teaspoon freshly ground black pepper

- 2 pounds London broil, top round or flank steak (about 1-inch thick)

Directions:

1. Combine the ketchup, honey, olive oil, apple cider vinegar, Worcestershire sauce, minced onion, paprika, salt and pepper in a small bowl and whisk together.

2. Generously pierce both sides of the meat with a fork or meat tenderizer and place it in a shallow dish. Pour the marinade mixture over the steak, making sure all sides of the meat get coated with the marinade. Cover and refrigerate overnight.

3. Preheat the air fryer to 400°F.

4. Transfer the London broil to the air fryer basket and air-fry for 28 minutes, depending on how rare or well done you like your steak. Flip the steak over halfway through the cooking time.

5. Remove the London broil from the air fryer and let it rest for five minutes on a cutting board. To serve, thinly slice the meat against the grain and transfer to a serving platter.

Crispy Ham And Eggs

Servings: 3
Cooking Time: 9 Minutes

Ingredients:

- 2 cups Rice-puff cereal, such as Rice Krispies
- ¼ cup Maple syrup
- ½ pound ¼- to ½-inch-thick ham steak (gluten-free, if a concern)
- 1 tablespoon Unsalted butter
- 3 Large eggs
- ⅛ teaspoon Table salt
- ⅛ teaspoon Ground black pepper

Directions:

1. Preheat the air fryer to 400°F.

2. Pour the cereal into a food processor, cover, and process until finely ground. Pour the ground cereal into a shallow soup plate or a small pie plate.

3. Smear the maple syrup on both sides of the ham, then set the ham into the ground cereal. Turn a few times, pressing gently, until evenly coated.

4. Set the ham steak in the basket and air-fry undisturbed for 5 minutes, or until browned.

5. Meanwhile, melt the butter in a medium or large nonstick skillet set over medium heat. Crack the eggs into the skillet and cook until the whites are set and the yolks are hot, about 3 minutes (or 4 minutes for a more set yolk.) Season with the salt and pepper.

6. When the ham is ready, transfer it to a serving platter, then slip the eggs from the skillet on top of it. Divide into portions to serve.

Steakhouse Filets Mignons

Servings: 3
Cooking Time: 12-15 Minutes

Ingredients:

- ¾ ounce Dried porcini mushrooms
- ¼ teaspoon Granulated white sugar
- ¼ teaspoon Ground white pepper
- ¼ teaspoon Table salt
- 6 ¼-pound filets mignons or beef tenderloin steaks
- 6 Thin-cut bacon strips (gluten-free, if a concern)

Directions:

1. Preheat the air fryer to 400°F.

2. Grind the dried mushrooms in a clean spice grinder until powdery. Add the sugar, white pepper, and salt. Grind to blend.

3. Rub this mushroom mixture into both cut sides of each filet. Wrap the circumference of each filet with a strip of bacon. (It will loop around the beef about 1½ times.)

4. Set the filets mignons in the basket on their sides with the bacon seam side down. Do not let the filets touch; keep at least ¼ inch open between them. Air-fry undisturbed for 12 minutes for rare, or until an instant-read meat thermometer inserted into the center of a filet registers 125°F (not USDA-approved); 13 minutes for medium-rare, or until an instant-read meat thermometer inserted into the center of a filet registers 132°F (not USDA-approved); or 15 minutes for medium, or until an instant-read meat thermometer inserted into the center of a filet registers 145°F (USDA-approved).

5. Use kitchen tongs to transfer the filets to a wire rack, setting them cut side down. Cool for 5 minutes before serving.

Beef And Spinach Braciole

Servings: 4
Cooking Time: 92 Minutes

Ingredients:
- 7-inch oven-safe baking pan or casserole
- ½ onion, finely chopped
- 1 teaspoon olive oil
- ⅓ cup red wine
- 2 cups crushed tomatoes
- 1 teaspoon Italian seasoning
- ½ teaspoon garlic powder
- ¼ teaspoon crushed red pepper flakes
- 2 tablespoons chopped fresh parsley
- 2 top round steaks (about 1½ pounds)
- salt and freshly ground black pepper
- 2 cups fresh spinach, chopped
- 1 clove minced garlic
- ½ cup roasted red peppers, julienned
- ½ cup grated pecorino cheese
- ¼ cup pine nuts, toasted and rough chopped
- 2 tablespoons olive oil

Directions:
1. Preheat the air fryer to 400°F.
2. Toss the onions and olive oil together in a 7-inch metal baking pan or casserole dish. Air-fry at 400°F for 5 minutes, stirring a couple times during the cooking process. Add the red wine, crushed tomatoes, Italian seasoning, garlic powder, red pepper flakes and parsley and stir. Cover the pan tightly with aluminum foil, lower the air fryer temperature to 350°F and continue to air-fry for 15 minutes.
3. While the sauce is simmering, prepare the beef. Using a meat mallet, pound the beef until it is ¼-inch thick. Season both sides of the beef with salt and pepper. Combine the spinach, garlic, red peppers, pecorino cheese, pine nuts and olive oil in a medium bowl. Season with salt and freshly ground black pepper. Spread the mixture evenly over the steaks. Starting at one of the short ends, roll the beef around the filling, tucking in the sides as you roll to ensure the filling is completely enclosed. Secure the beef rolls with toothpicks.
4. Remove the baking pan with the sauce from the air fryer and set it aside. Preheat the air fryer to 400°F.
5. Brush or spray the beef rolls with a little olive oil and air-fry at 400°F for 12 minutes, rotating the beef during the cooking process for even browning. When the beef is browned, submerge the rolls into the sauce in the baking pan, cover

the pan with foil and return it to the air fryer. Air-fry at 250°F for 60 minutes.

6. Remove the beef rolls from the sauce. Cut each roll into slices and serve with pasta, ladling some of the sauce overtop.

Air-fried Roast Beef With Rosemary Roasted Potatoes

Servings: 8
Cooking Time: 60 Minutes

Ingredients:
- 1 (5-pound) top sirloin roast
- salt and freshly ground black pepper
- 1 teaspoon dried thyme
- 2 pounds red potatoes, halved or quartered
- 2 teaspoons olive oil
- 1 teaspoon very finely chopped fresh rosemary, plus more for garnish

Directions:
1. Start by making sure your roast will fit into the air fryer basket without touching the top element. Trim it if you have to in order to get it to fit nicely in your air fryer. (You can always save the trimmings for another use, like a beef sandwich.)
2. Preheat the air fryer to 360°F.
3. Season the beef all over with salt, pepper and thyme. Transfer the seasoned roast to the air fryer basket.
4. Air-fry at 360°F for 20 minutes. Turn the roast over and continue to air-fry at 360°F for another 20 minutes.
5. Toss the potatoes with the olive oil, salt, pepper and fresh rosemary. Turn the roast over again in the air fryer basket and toss the potatoes in around the sides of the roast. Air-fry the roast and potatoes at 360°F for another 20 minutes.

Check the internal temperature of the roast with an instant-read thermometer, and continue to roast until the beef is 5° lower than your desired degree of doneness. (Rare – 130°F, Medium – 150°F, Well done – 170°F.) Let the roast rest for 5 to 10 minutes before slicing and serving. While the roast is resting, continue to air-fry the potatoes if desired for extra browning and crispiness.

6. Slice the roast and serve with the potatoes, adding a little more fresh rosemary if desired.

Vietnamese Shaking Beef

Servings: 3
Cooking Time: 7 Minutes

Ingredients:
- 1 pound Beef tenderloin, cut into 1-inch cubes
- 1 tablespoon Regular or low-sodium soy sauce or gluten-free tamari sauce
- 1 tablespoon Fish sauce (gluten-free, if a concern)
- 1 tablespoon Dark brown sugar
- 1½ teaspoons Ground black pepper
- 3 Medium scallions, trimmed and thinly sliced
- 2 tablespoons Butter
- 1½ teaspoons Minced garlic

Directions:
1. Mix the beef, soy or tamari sauce, fish sauce, and brown sugar in a bowl until well combined. Cover and refrigerate for at least 2 hours or up to 8 hours, tossing the beef at least twice in the marinade.
2. Put a 6-inch round or square cake pan in an air-fryer basket for a small batch, a 7-inch round or square cake pan for a medium batch, or an 8-

inch round or square cake pan for a large one. Or put one of these on the rack of a toaster oven–style air fryer. Heat the machine with the pan in it to 400°F. When the machine it at temperature, let the pan sit in the heat for 2 to 3 minutes so that it gets very hot.

3. Use a slotted spoon to transfer the beef to the pan, leaving any marinade behind in the bowl. Spread the meat into as close to an even layer as you can. Air-fry undisturbed for 5 minutes. Meanwhile, discard the marinade, if any.

4. Add the scallions, butter, and garlic to the beef. Air-fry for 2 minutes, tossing and rearranging the beef and scallions repeatedly, perhaps every 20 seconds.

5. Remove the basket from the machine and let the meat cool in the pan for a couple of minutes before serving.

Lamb Chops

Servings: 2
Cooking Time: 20 Minutes

Ingredients:

- 2 teaspoons oil
- ½ teaspoon ground rosemary
- ½ teaspoon lemon juice
- 1 pound lamb chops, approximately 1-inch thick
- salt and pepper
- cooking spray

Directions:

1. Mix the oil, rosemary, and lemon juice together and rub into all sides of the lamb chops. Season to taste with salt and pepper.

2. For best flavor, cover lamb chops and allow them to rest in the fridge for 20 minutes.

3. Spray air fryer basket with nonstick spray and place lamb chops in it.

4. Cook at 360°F for approximately 20minutes. This will cook chops to medium. The meat will be juicy but have no remaining pink. Cook for a minute or two longer for well done chops. For rare chops, stop cooking after about 12minutes and check for doneness.

Bread And Breakfast

Wild Blueberry Lemon Chia Bread

Servings: 6

Cooking Time: 27 Minutes

Ingredients:

- ¼ cup extra-virgin olive oil
- ⅓ cup plus 1 tablespoon cane sugar
- 1 large egg
- 3 tablespoons fresh lemon juice
- 1 tablespoon lemon zest
- ⅔ cup milk
- 1 cup all-purpose flour
- ¾ teaspoon baking powder
- ⅛ teaspoon salt
- 2 tablespoons chia seeds
- 1 cup frozen wild blueberries
- ⅓ cup powdered sugar
- 2 teaspoons milk

Directions:

1. Preheat the air fryer to 310°F.

2. In a medium bowl, mix the olive oil with the sugar. Whisk in the egg, lemon juice, lemon zest, and milk; set aside.

3. In a small bowl, combine the all-purpose flour, baking powder, and salt.

4. Slowly mix the dry ingredients into the wet ingredients. Stir in the chia seeds and wild blueberries.

5. Liberally spray a 7-inch springform pan with olive-oil spray. Pour the batter into the pan and place the pan in the air fryer. Bake for 25 to 27 minutes, or until a toothpick inserted in the center comes out clean.

6. Remove and let cool on a wire rack for 10 minutes prior to removing from the pan.

7. Meanwhile, in a small bowl, mix the powdered sugar with the milk to create the glaze.

8. Slice and serve with a drizzle of the powdered sugar glaze.

White Wheat Walnut Bread

Servings: 8

Cooking Time: 25 Minutes

Ingredients:

- 1 cup lukewarm water (105–115°F)
- 1 packet RapidRise yeast
- 1 tablespoon light brown sugar
- 2 cups whole-grain white wheat flour
- 1 egg, room temperature, beaten with a fork
- 2 teaspoons olive oil
- ½ teaspoon salt
- ½ cup chopped walnuts
- cooking spray

Directions:

1. In a small bowl, mix the water, yeast, and brown sugar.

2. Pour yeast mixture over flour and mix until smooth.

3. Add the egg, olive oil, and salt and beat with a wooden spoon for 2minutes.

4. Stir in chopped walnuts. You will have very thick batter rather than stiff bread dough.

5. Spray air fryer baking pan with cooking spray and pour in batter, smoothing the top.

6. Let batter rise for 15minutes.

7. Preheat air fryer to 360°F.

8. Cook bread for 25 minutes, until toothpick pushed into center comes out with crumbs clinging. Let bread rest for 10minutes before removing from pan.

Brown Sugar Grapefruit

Servings: 2

Cooking Time: 4 Minutes

Ingredients:

- 1 grapefruit
- 2 to 4 teaspoons brown sugar

Directions:

1. Preheat the air fryer to 400°F.
2. While the air fryer is Preheating, cut the grapefruit in half horizontally (in other words not through the stem or blossom end of the grapefruit). Slice the bottom of the grapefruit to help it sit flat on the counter if necessary. Using a sharp paring knife (serrated is great), cut around the grapefruit between the flesh of the fruit and the peel. Then, cut each segment away from the membrane so that it is sitting freely in the fruit.
3. Sprinkle 1 to 2 teaspoons of brown sugar on each half of the prepared grapefruit. Set up a rack in the air fryer basket (use an air fryer rack or make your own rack with some crumpled up aluminum foil). You don't have to use a rack, but doing so will get the grapefruit closer to the element so that the brown sugar can caramelize a little better. Transfer the grapefruit half to the rack in the air fryer basket. Depending on how big your grapefruit are and what size air fryer you have, you may need to do each half separately to make sure they sit flat.
4. Air-fry at 400°F for 4 minutes.
5. Remove and let it cool for just a minute before enjoying.

Goat Cheese, Beet, And Kale Frittata

Servings: 6

Cooking Time: 20 Minutes

Ingredients:

- 6 large eggs
- ½ teaspoon garlic powder
- ¼ teaspoon black pepper
- ¼ teaspoon salt
- 1 cup chopped kale
- 1 cup cooked and chopped red beets
- ⅓ cup crumbled goat cheese

Directions:

1. Preheat the air fryer to 320°F.
2. In a medium bowl, whisk the eggs with the garlic powder, pepper, and salt. Mix in the kale, beets, and goat cheese.
3. Spray an oven-safe 7-inch springform pan with cooking spray. Pour the egg mixture into the pan and place it in the air fryer basket.
4. Cook for 20 minutes, or until the internal temperature reaches 145°F.
5. When the frittata is cooked, let it set for 5 minutes before removing from the pan.
6. Slice and serve immediately.

Sweet Potato-cinnamon Toast

Servings: 6

Cooking Time: 8 Minutes

Ingredients:

- 1 small sweet potato, cut into ⅜-inch slices
- oil for misting
- ground cinnamon

Directions:

1. Preheat air fryer to 390°F.
2. Spray both sides of sweet potato slices with oil. Sprinkle both sides with cinnamon to taste.
3. Place potato slices in air fryer basket in a single layer.

4. Cook for 4minutes, turn, and cook for 4 more minutes or until potato slices are barely fork tender.

Pepperoni Pizza Bread

Servings: 4
Cooking Time: 15 Minutes

Ingredients:
- 7-inch round bread boule
- 2 cups grated mozzarella cheese
- 1 tablespoon dried oregano
- 1 cup pizza sauce
- 1 cup mini pepperoni or pepperoni slices, cut in quarters
- Pizza sauce for dipping (optional)

Directions:
1. Make 7 to 8 deep slices across the bread boule, leaving 1 inch of bread uncut at the bottom of every slice before you reach the cutting board. The slices should go about three quarters of the way through the boule and be about 2 inches apart from each other. Turn the bread boule 90 degrees and make 7 to 8 similar slices perpendicular to the first slices to form squares in the bread. Again, make sure you don't cut all the way through the bread.
2. Combine the mozzarella cheese and oregano in a small bowl.
3. Fill the slices in the bread with pizza sauce by gently spreading the bread apart and spooning the sauce in between the squares of bread. Top the sauce with the mozzarella cheese mixture and then the pepperoni. Do your very best to get the cheese and pepperoni in between the slices, rather than on top of the bread. Keep spreading the bread apart and stuffing the ingredients in, but be careful not to tear the bottom of the bread.

4. Preheat the air fryer to 320°F.
5. Transfer the bread boule to the air fryer basket and air-fry for 15 minutes, making sure the top doesn't get too dark. (It will just be the cheese on top that gets dark, so if you've done a good job of tucking the cheese in between the slices, this shouldn't be an issue.)
6. Carefully remove the bread from the basket with a spatula. Transfer it to a serving platter with more sauce to dip into if desired. Serve with a lot of napkins so that people can just pull the bread apart with their hands and enjoy!

Orange Rolls

Servings: 8
Cooking Time: 10 Minutes

Ingredients:
- parchment paper
- 3 ounces low-fat cream cheese
- 1 tablespoon low-fat sour cream or plain yogurt (not Greek yogurt)
- 2 teaspoons sugar
- ¼ teaspoon pure vanilla extract
- ¼ teaspoon orange extract
- 1 can (8 count) organic crescent roll dough
- ¼ cup chopped walnuts
- ¼ cup dried cranberries
- ¼ cup shredded, sweetened coconut
- butter-flavored cooking spray
- Orange Glaze
- ½ cup powdered sugar
- 1 tablespoon orange juice
- ¼ teaspoon orange extract
- dash of salt

Directions:

1. Cut a circular piece of parchment paper slightly smaller than the bottom of your air fryer basket. Set aside.

2. In a small bowl, combine the cream cheese, sour cream or yogurt, sugar, and vanilla and orange extracts. Stir until smooth.

3. Preheat air fryer to 300°F.

4. Separate crescent roll dough into 8 triangles and divide cream cheese mixture among them. Starting at wide end, spread cheese mixture to within 1 inch of point.

5. Sprinkle nuts and cranberries evenly over cheese mixture.

6. Starting at wide end, roll up triangles, then sprinkle with coconut, pressing in lightly to make it stick. Spray tops of rolls with butter-flavored cooking spray.

7. Place parchment paper in air fryer basket, and place 4 rolls on top, spaced evenly.

8. Cook for 10minutes, until rolls are golden brown and cooked through.

9. Repeat steps 7 and 8 to cook remaining 4 rolls. You should be able to use the same piece of parchment paper twice.

10. In a small bowl, stir together ingredients for glaze and drizzle over warm rolls.

Crispy Bacon

Servings: 6
Cooking Time: 20 Minutes

Ingredients:

- 12 ounces bacon

Directions:

1. Preheat the air fryer to 350°F for 3 minutes.

2. Lay out the bacon in a single layer, slightly overlapping the strips of bacon.

3. Air fry for 10 minutes or until desired crispness.

4. Repeat until all the bacon has been cooked.

French Toast Sticks

Servings: 4
Cooking Time: 7 Minutes

Ingredients:

- 2 eggs
- ½ cup milk
- ⅛ teaspoon salt
- ½ teaspoon pure vanilla extract
- ¾ cup crushed cornflakes
- 6 slices sandwich bread, each slice cut into 4 strips
- oil for misting or cooking spray
- maple syrup or honey

Directions:

1. In a small bowl, beat together eggs, milk, salt, and vanilla.

2. Place crushed cornflakes on a plate or in a shallow dish.

3. Dip bread strips in egg mixture, shake off excess, and roll in cornflake crumbs.

4. Spray both sides of bread strips with oil.

5. Place bread strips in air fryer basket in single layer.

6. Cook at 390°F for 7minutes or until they're dark golden brown.

7. Repeat steps 5 and 6 to cook remaining French toast sticks.

8. Serve with maple syrup or honey for dipping.

Hashbrown Potatoes Lyonnaise

Servings: 4
Cooking Time: 33 Minutes

Ingredients:

- 1 Vidalia (or other sweet) onion, sliced
- 1 teaspoon butter, melted
- 1 teaspoon brown sugar
- 2 large russet potatoes (about 1 pound), sliced ½-inch thick
- 1 tablespoon vegetable oil
- salt and freshly ground black pepper

Directions:

1. Preheat the air fryer to 370°F.
2. Toss the sliced onions, melted butter and brown sugar together in the air fryer basket. Air-fry for 8 minutes, shaking the basket occasionally to help the onions cook evenly.
3. While the onions are cooking, bring a 3-quart saucepan of salted water to a boil on the stovetop. Par-cook the potatoes in boiling water for 3 minutes. Drain the potatoes and pat them dry with a clean kitchen towel.
4. Add the potatoes to the onions in the air fryer basket and drizzle with vegetable oil. Toss to coat the potatoes with the oil and season with salt and freshly ground black pepper.
5. Increase the air fryer temperature to 400°F and air-fry for 22 minutes tossing the vegetables a few times during the cooking time to help the potatoes brown evenly. Season to taste again with salt and freshly ground black pepper and serve warm.

Bacon, Broccoli And Swiss Cheese Bread Pudding

Servings: 2
Cooking Time: 48 Minutes

Ingredients:

- ½ pound thick cut bacon, cut into ¼-inch pieces
- 3 cups brioche bread or rolls, cut into ½-inch cubes
- 3 eggs
- 1 cup milk
- ½ teaspoon salt
- freshly ground black pepper
- 1 cup frozen broccoli florets, thawed and chopped
- 1½ cups grated Swiss cheese

Directions:

1. Preheat the air fryer to 400°F.
2. Air-fry the bacon for 6 minutes until crispy, shaking the basket a few times while it cooks to help it cook evenly. Remove the bacon and set it aside on a paper towel.
3. Air-fry the brioche bread cubes for 2 minutes to dry and toast lightly. (If your brioche is a few days old and slightly stale, you can omit this step.)
4. Butter a 6- or 7-inch cake pan. Combine all the ingredients in a large bowl and toss well. Transfer the mixture to the buttered cake pan, cover with aluminum foil and refrigerate the bread pudding overnight, or for at least 8 hours.
5. Remove the casserole from the refrigerator an hour before you plan to cook, and let it sit on the countertop to come to room temperature.
6. Preheat the air fryer to 330°F. Transfer the covered cake pan, to the basket of the air fryer, lowering the dish into the basket using a sling made of aluminum foil (fold a piece of aluminum foil into a strip about 2-inches wide by 24-inches long). Fold the ends of the aluminum foil over the top of the dish before returning the basket to

the air fryer. Air-fry for 20 minutes. Remove the foil and air-fry for an additional 20 minutes. If the top starts to brown a little too much before the custard has set, simply return the foil to the pan. The bread pudding has cooked through when a skewer inserted into the center comes out clean.

Crustless Broccoli, Roasted Pepper And Fontina Quiche

Servings: 4
Cooking Time: 60 Minutes

Ingredients:
- 7-inch cake pan
- 1 cup broccoli florets
- ¾ cup chopped roasted red peppers
- 1¼ cups grated Fontina cheese
- 6 eggs
- ¾ cup heavy cream
- ½ teaspoon salt
- freshly ground black pepper

Directions:
1. Preheat the air fryer to 360°F.
2. Grease the inside of a 7-inch cake pan (4 inches deep) or other oven-safe pan that will fit into your air fryer. Place the broccoli florets and roasted red peppers in the cake pan and top with the grated Fontina cheese.
3. Whisk the eggs and heavy cream together in a bowl. Season the eggs with salt and freshly ground black pepper. Pour the egg mixture over the cheese and vegetables and cover the pan with aluminum foil. Transfer the cake pan to the air fryer basket.
4. Air-fry at 360°F for 60 minutes. Remove the aluminum foil for the last two minutes of cooking time.

5. Unmold the quiche onto a platter and cut it into slices to serve with a side salad or perhaps some air-fried potatoes.

Ham And Cheddar Gritters

Servings: 6
Cooking Time: 12 Minutes

Ingredients:
- 4 cups water
- 1 cup quick-cooking grits
- ¼ teaspoon salt
- 2 tablespoons butter
- 2 cups grated Cheddar cheese, divided
- 1 cup finely diced ham
- 1 tablespoon chopped chives
- salt and freshly ground black pepper
- 1 egg, beaten
- 2 cups panko breadcrumbs
- vegetable oil

Directions:
1. Bring the water to a boil in a saucepan. Whisk in the grits and ¼ teaspoon of salt, and cook for 7 minutes until the grits are soft. Remove the pan from the heat and stir in the butter and 1 cup of the grated Cheddar cheese. Transfer the grits to a bowl and let them cool for just 10 to 15 minutes.
2. Stir the ham, chives and the rest of the cheese into the grits and season with salt and pepper to taste. Add the beaten egg and refrigerate the mixture for 30 minutes. (Try not to chill the grits much longer than 30 minutes, or the mixture will be too firm to shape into patties.)
3. While the grit mixture is chilling, make the country gravy and set it aside.
4. Place the panko breadcrumbs in a shallow dish. Measure out ¼-cup portions of the grits mixture and shape them into patties. Coat all

sides of the patties with the panko breadcrumbs, patting them with your hands so the crumbs adhere to the patties. You should have about 16 patties. Spray both sides of the patties with oil.

5. Preheat the air fryer to 400°F.

6. In batches of 5 or 6, air-fry the fritters for 8 minutes. Using a flat spatula, flip the fritters over and air-fry for another 4 minutes.

7. Serve hot with country gravy.

Bacon Puff Pastry Pinwheels

Servings: 8

Cooking Time: 10 Minutes

Ingredients:

- 1 sheet of puff pastry
- 2 tablespoons maple syrup
- ¼ cup brown sugar
- 8 slices bacon (not thick cut)
- coarsely cracked black pepper
- vegetable oil

Directions:

1. On a lightly floured surface, roll the puff pastry out into a square that measures roughly 10 inches wide by however long your bacon strips are (usually about 11 inches). Cut the pastry into eight even strips.

2. Brush the strips of pastry with the maple syrup and sprinkle the brown sugar on top, leaving 1 inch of dough exposed at the far end of each strip. Place a slice of bacon on each strip of puff pastry, letting 1/8-inch of the length of bacon hang over the edge of the pastry. Season generously with coarsely ground black pepper.

3. With the exposed end of the pastry strips away from you, roll the bacon and pastry strips up into pinwheels. Dab a little water on the exposed

end of the pastry and pinch it to the pinwheel to seal the pastry shut.

4. Preheat the air fryer to 360°F.

5. Brush or spray the air fryer basket with a little vegetable oil. Place the pinwheels into the basket and air-fry at 360°F for 8 minutes. Turn the pinwheels over and air-fry for another 2 minutes to brown the bottom. Serve warm.

Hush Puffins

Servings: 20

Cooking Time: 8 Minutes

Ingredients:

- 1 cup buttermilk
- ¼ cup butter, melted
- 2 eggs
- 1½ cups all-purpose flour
- 1½ cups cornmeal
- ⅓ cup sugar
- 1 teaspoon baking soda
- 1 teaspoon salt
- 4 scallions, minced
- vegetable oil

Directions:

1. Combine the buttermilk, butter and eggs in a large mixing bowl. In a second bowl combine the flour, cornmeal, sugar, baking soda and salt. Add the dry ingredients to the wet ingredients, stirring just to combine. Stir in the minced scallions and refrigerate the batter for 30 minutes.

2. Shape the batter into 2-inch balls. Brush or spray the balls with oil.

3. Preheat the air fryer to 360°F.

4. Air-fry the hush puffins in two batches at 360°F for 8 minutes, turning them over after 6 minutes of the cooking process.

5. Serve warm with butter.

Roasted Tomato And Cheddar Rolls

Servings: 12

Cooking Time: 55 Minutes

Ingredients:

- 4 Roma tomatoes
- ½ clove garlic, minced
- 1 tablespoon olive oil
- ¼ teaspoon dried thyme
- salt and freshly ground black pepper
- 4 cups all-purpose flour
- 1 teaspoon active dry yeast
- 2 teaspoons sugar
- 2 teaspoons salt
- 1 tablespoon olive oil
- 1 cup grated Cheddar cheese, plus more for sprinkling at the end
- 1½ cups water

Directions:

1. Cut the Roma tomatoes in half, remove the seeds with your fingers and transfer to a bowl. Add the garlic, olive oil, dried thyme, salt and freshly ground black pepper and toss well.

2. Preheat the air fryer to 390°F.

3. Place the tomatoes, cut side up in the air fryer basket and air-fry for 10 minutes. The tomatoes should just start to brown. Shake the basket to redistribute the tomatoes, and air-fry for another 5 to 10 minutes at 330°F until the tomatoes are no longer juicy. Let the tomatoes cool and then rough chop them.

4. Combine the flour, yeast, sugar and salt in the bowl of a stand mixer. Add the olive oil, chopped roasted tomatoes and Cheddar cheese to the flour mixture and start to mix using the dough hook attachment. As you're mixing, add 1¼ cups of the water, mixing until the dough comes together. Continue to knead the dough with the dough hook for another 10 minutes, adding enough water to the dough to get it to the right consistency.

5. Transfer the dough to an oiled bowl, cover with a clean kitchen towel and let it rest and rise until it has doubled in volume – about 1 to 2 hours. Then, divide the dough into 12 equal portions. Roll each portion of dough into a ball. Lightly coat each dough ball with oil and let the dough balls rest and rise a second time, covered lightly with plastic wrap for 45 minutes. (Alternately, you can place the rolls in the refrigerator overnight and take them out 2 hours before you bake them.)

6. Preheat the air fryer to 360°F.

7. Spray the dough balls and the air fryer basket with a little olive oil. Place three rolls at a time in the basket and bake for 10 minutes. Add a little grated Cheddar cheese on top of the rolls for the last 2 minutes of air frying for an attractive finish.

Scones

Servings: 9

Cooking Time: 8 Minutes Per Batch

Ingredients:

- 2 cups self-rising flour, plus ¼ cup for kneading
- ⅓ cup granulated sugar
- ¼ cup butter, cold
- 1 cup milk

Directions:

1. Preheat air fryer at 360°F.

2. In large bowl, stir together flour and sugar.

3. Cut cold butter into tiny cubes, and stir into flour mixture with fork.

4. Stir in milk until soft dough forms.

5. Sprinkle ¼ cup of flour onto wax paper and place dough on top. Knead lightly by folding and turning the dough about 6 to 8 times.

6. Pat dough into a 6 x 6-inch square.

7. Cut into 9 equal squares.

8. Place all squares in air fryer basket or as many as will fit in a single layer, close together but not touching.

9. Cook at 360°F for 8minutes. When done, scones will be lightly browned on top and will spring back when pressed gently with a dull knife.

10. Repeat steps 8 and 9 to cook remaining scones.

Spinach And Artichoke White Pizza

Servings: 2
Cooking Time: 18 Minutes

Ingredients:
- olive oil
- 3 cups fresh spinach
- 2 cloves garlic, minced, divided
- 1 (6- to 8-ounce) pizza dough ball*
- ½ cup grated mozzarella cheese
- ¼ cup grated Fontina cheese
- ¼ cup artichoke hearts, coarsely chopped
- 2 tablespoons grated Parmesan cheese
- ¼ teaspoon dried oregano
- salt and freshly ground black pepper

Directions:
1. Heat the oil in a medium sauté pan on the stovetop. Add the spinach and half the minced garlic to the pan and sauté for a few minutes, until the spinach has wilted. Remove the sautéed spinach from the pan and set it aside.

2. Preheat the air fryer to 390°F.

3. Cut out a piece of aluminum foil the same size as the bottom of the air fryer basket. Brush the foil circle with olive oil. Shape the dough into a circle and place it on top of the foil. Dock the dough by piercing it several times with a fork. Brush the dough lightly with olive oil and transfer it into the air fryer basket with the foil on the bottom.

4. Air-fry the plain pizza dough for 6 minutes. Turn the dough over, remove the aluminum foil and brush again with olive oil. Air-fry for an additional 4 minutes.

5. Sprinkle the mozzarella and Fontina cheeses over the dough. Top with the spinach and artichoke hearts. Sprinkle the Parmesan cheese and dried oregano on top and drizzle with olive oil. Lower the temperature of the air fryer to 350°F and cook for 8 minutes, until the cheese has melted and is lightly browned. Season to taste with salt and freshly ground black pepper.

Cajun Breakfast Potatoes

Servings: 4
Cooking Time: 20 Minutes

Ingredients:
- 1 pound roasting potatoes (like russet), scrubbed clean
- 1 tablespoon vegetable oil
- 2 teaspoons paprika
- ½ teaspoon garlic powder
- ¼ teaspoon onion powder
- ¼ teaspoon ground cumin
- 1 teaspoon thyme
- 1 teaspoon sea salt
- ½ teaspoon black pepper

Directions:
1. Cut the potatoes into 1-inch cubes.

2. In a large bowl, toss the cut potatoes with vegetable oil.

3. Sprinkle paprika, garlic powder, onion powder, cumin, thyme, salt, and pepper onto the potatoes, and toss to coat well.

4. Preheat the air fryer to 400°F for 4 minutes.

5. Add the potatoes to the air fryer basket and bake for 10 minutes. Stir or toss the potatoes and continue baking for an additional 5 minutes. Stir or toss again and continue baking for an additional 5 minutes or until the desired crispness is achieved.

Zucchini Walnut Bread

Servings: 6
Cooking Time: 30 Minutes

Ingredients:
- ¾ cup all-purpose flour
- ½ teaspoon baking soda
- 1 teaspoon ground cinnamon
- ⅛ teaspoon salt
- 1 large egg
- ⅓ cup packed brown sugar
- ¼ cup canola oil
- 1 teaspoon vanilla extract
- ⅓ cup milk
- 1 medium zucchini, shredded (about 1⅓ cups)
- ⅓ cup chopped walnuts

Directions:
1. Preheat the air fryer to 320°F.

2. In a medium bowl, mix together the flour, baking soda, cinnamon, and salt.

3. In a large bowl, whisk together the egg, brown sugar, oil, vanilla, and milk. Stir in the zucchini.

4. Slowly fold the dry ingredients into the wet ingredients. Stir in the chopped walnuts. Then pour the batter into two 4-inch oven-safe loaf pans.

5. Bake for 30 minutes or until a toothpick inserted into the center comes out clean. Let cool before slicing.

6. NOTE: Store tightly wrapped on the counter for up to 5 days, in the refrigerator for up to 10 days, or in the freezer for 3 months.

Spinach-bacon Rollups

Servings: 4
Cooking Time: 9 Minutes

Ingredients:
- 4 flour tortillas (6- or 7-inch size)
- 4 slices Swiss cheese
- 1 cup baby spinach leaves
- 4 slices turkey bacon

Directions:
1. Preheat air fryer to 390°F.

2. On each tortilla, place one slice of cheese and ¼ cup of spinach.

3. Roll up tortillas and wrap each with a strip of bacon. Secure each end with a toothpick.

4. Place rollups in air fryer basket, leaving a little space in between them.

5. Cook for 4minutes. Turn and rearrange rollups (for more even cooking) and cook for 5minutes longer, until bacon is crisp.

Apple Fritters

Servings: 6
Cooking Time: 12 Minutes

Ingredients:
- 1 cup all-purpose flour
- 1½ teaspoons baking powder
- ¼ teaspoon salt
- 2 tablespoon brown sugar
- 1 teaspoon vanilla extract
- ¾ cup plain Greek yogurt

- 1 tablespoon cinnamon
- 1 large Granny Smith apple, cored, peeled, and finely chopped
- ¼ cup chopped walnuts
- ½ cup powdered sugar
- 1 tablespoon milk

Directions:

1. Preheat the air fryer to 320°F.
2. In a medium bowl, combine the flour, baking powder, and salt.
3. In a large bowl, add the brown sugar, vanilla, yogurt, cinnamon, apples, and walnuts. Mix the dry ingredients into the wet, using your hands to combine, until all the ingredients are mixed together. Knead the mixture in the bowl about 4 times.
4. Lightly spray the air fryer basket with olive oil spray.
5. Divide the batter into 6 equally sized balls; then lightly flatten them and place inside the basket. Repeat until all the fritters are formed.
6. Place the basket in the air fryer and cook for 6 minutes, flip, and then cook another 6 minutes.
7. While the fritters are cooking, in a small bowl, mix the powdered sugar with the milk. Set aside.
8. When the cooking completes, remove the air fryer basket and allow the fritters to cool on a wire rack. Drizzle with the homemade glaze and serve.

Pancake Muffins

Servings: 4
Cooking Time: 8 Minutes

Ingredients:

- 1 cup flour
- 2 tablespoons sugar (optional)
- ½ teaspoon baking soda
- 1 teaspoon baking powder
- ¼ teaspoon salt
- 1 egg, beaten
- 1 cup buttermilk
- 2 tablespoons melted butter
- 1 teaspoon pure vanilla extract
- 24 foil muffin cups
- cooking spray
- Suggested Fillings
- 1 teaspoon of jelly or fruit preserves
- 1 tablespoon or less fresh blueberries; chopped fresh strawberries; chopped frozen cherries; dark chocolate chips; chopped walnuts, pecans, or other nuts; cooked, crumbled bacon or sausage

Directions:

1. In a large bowl, stir together flour, optional sugar, baking soda, baking powder, and salt.
2. In a small bowl, combine egg, buttermilk, butter, and vanilla. Mix well.
3. Pour egg mixture into dry ingredients and stir to mix well but don't overbeat.
4. Double up the muffin cups and remove the paper liners from the top cups. Spray the foil cups lightly with cooking spray.
5. Place 6 sets of muffin cups in air fryer basket. Pour just enough batter into each cup to cover the bottom. Sprinkle with desired filling. Pour in more batter to cover the filling and fill the cups about ¾ full.
6. Cook at 330°F for 8minutes.
7. Repeat steps 5 and 6 for the remaining 6 pancake muffins.

Desserts And Sweets

Boston Cream Donut Holes

Servings: 24

Cooking Time: 12 Minutes

Ingredients:

- 1½ cups bread flour
- 1 teaspoon active dry yeast
- 1 tablespoon sugar
- ¼ teaspoon salt
- ½ cup warm milk
- ½ teaspoon pure vanilla extract
- 2 egg yolks
- 2 tablespoons butter, melted
- vegetable oil
- Custard Filling:
- 1 (3.4-ounce) box French vanilla instant pudding mix
- ¾ cup whole milk
- ¼ cup heavy cream
- Chocolate Glaze:
- 1 cup chocolate chips
- ⅓ cup heavy cream

Directions:

1. Combine the flour, yeast, sugar and salt in the bowl of a stand mixer. Add the milk, vanilla, egg yolks and butter. Mix until the dough starts to come together in a ball. Transfer the dough to a floured surface and knead the dough by hand for 2 minutes. Shape the dough into a ball, place it in a large oiled bowl, cover the bowl with a clean kitchen towel and let the dough rise for 1 to 1½ hours or until the dough has doubled in size.

2. When the dough has risen, punch it down and roll it into a 24-inch log. Cut the dough into 24 pieces and roll each piece into a ball. Place the dough balls on a baking sheet and let them rise for another 30 minutes.

3. Preheat the air fryer to 400°F.

4. Spray or brush the dough balls lightly with vegetable oil and air-fry eight at a time for 4 minutes, turning them over halfway through the cooking time.

5. While donut holes are cooking, make the filling and chocolate glaze. To make the filling, use an electric hand mixer to beat the French vanilla pudding, milk and ¼ cup of heavy cream together for 2 minutes.

6. To make the chocolate glaze, place the chocolate chips in a medium-sized bowl. Bring the heavy cream to a boil on the stovetop and pour it over the chocolate chips. Stir until the chips are melted and the glaze is smooth.

7. To fill the donut holes, place the custard filling in a pastry bag with a long tip. Poke a hole into the side of the donut hole with a small knife. Wiggle the knife around to make room for the filling. Place the pastry bag tip into the hole and slowly squeeze the custard into the center of the donut. Dip the top half of the donut into the chocolate glaze, letting any excess glaze drip back into the bowl. Let the glazed donut holes sit for a few minutes before serving.

Fried Twinkies

Servings:6

Cooking Time: 5 Minutes

Ingredients:

- 2 Large egg white(s)
- 2 tablespoons Water
- 1½ cups (about 9 ounces) Ground gingersnap cookie crumbs
- 6 Twinkies
- Vegetable oil spray

Directions:

1. Preheat the air fryer to 400°F.

2. Set up and fill two shallow soup plates or small pie plates on your counter: one for the egg white(s), whisked with the water until foamy; and one for the gingersnap crumbs.

3. Dip a Twinkie in the egg white(s), turning it to coat on all sides, even the ends. Let the excess egg white mixture slip back into the rest, then set the Twinkie in the crumbs. Roll it to coat on all sides, even the ends, pressing gently to get an even coating. Then repeat this process: egg white(s), followed by crumbs. Lightly coat the prepared Twinkie on all sides with vegetable oil spray. Set aside and coat each of the remaining Twinkies with the same double-dipping technique, followed by spraying.

4. Set the Twinkies flat side up in the basket with as much air space between them as possible. Air-fry for 5 minutes, or until browned and crunchy.

5. Use a nonstick-safe spatula to gently transfer the Twinkies to a wire rack. Cool for at least 10 minutes before serving.

Caramel Apple Crumble

Servings: 6

Cooking Time: 50 Minutes

Ingredients:

- 4 apples, peeled and thinly sliced
- 2 tablespoons sugar
- 1 tablespoon flour
- 1 teaspoon ground cinnamon
- ¼ teaspoon ground allspice
- healthy pinch ground nutmeg
- 10 caramel squares, cut into small pieces
- Crumble Topping:
- ¾ cup rolled oats
- ¼ cup sugar
- ⅓ cup flour
- ¼ teaspoon ground cinnamon
- 6 tablespoons butter, melted

Directions:

1. Preheat the air fryer to 330°F.

2. Combine the apples, sugar, flour, and spices in a large bowl and toss to coat. Add the caramel pieces and mix well. Pour the apple mixture into a 1-quart round baking dish that will fit in your air fryer basket (6-inch diameter).

3. To make the crumble topping, combine the rolled oats, sugar, flour and cinnamon in a small bowl. Add the melted butter and mix well. Top the apples with the crumble mixture. Cover the entire dish with aluminum foil and transfer the dish to the air fryer basket, lowering the dish into the basket using a sling made of aluminum foil (fold a piece of aluminum foil into a strip about 2-inches wide by 24-inches long). Fold the ends of the aluminum foil over the top of the dish before returning the basket to the air fryer.

4. Air-fry at 330°F for 25 minutes. Remove the aluminum foil and continue to air-fry for another 25 minutes. Serve the crumble warm with whipped cream or vanilla ice cream, if desired.

Air-fried Strawberry Hand Tarts

Servings: 9

Cooking Time: 9 Minutes

Ingredients:

- ½ cup butter, softened
- ½ cup sugar
- 2 eggs
- 1 teaspoon vanilla extract
- 2 tablespoons lemon zest
- 2½ cups all-purpose flour
- 1 teaspoon baking powder
- ¼ teaspoon salt
- 1¼ cups strawberry jam, divided
- 1 egg white, beaten
- 1 cup powdered sugar
- 2 teaspoons milk

Directions:

1. Combine the butter and sugar in a bowl and beat with an electric mixer until the mixture is light and fluffy. Add the eggs one at a time. Add the vanilla extract and lemon zest and mix well. In a separate bowl, combine the flour, baking powder and salt. Add the dry ingredients to the wet ingredients, mixing just until the dough comes together. Transfer the dough to a floured surface and knead by hand for 10 minutes. Cover with a clean kitchen towel and let the dough rest for 30 minutes. (Alternatively, dough can be mixed and kneaded in a stand mixer.)

2. Divide the dough in half and roll each half out into a ¼-inch thick rectangle that measures 12-inches x 9-inches. Cut each rectangle of dough into nine 4-inch x 3-inch rectangles (a pizza cutter is very helpful for this task). You should have 18 rectangles. Spread two teaspoons of strawberry jam in the center of nine of the rectangles leaving a ¼-inch border around the edges. Brush the egg white around the edges of each rectangle and top with the remaining nine rectangles of dough. Press the back of a fork around the edges to seal the tarts shut. Brush the top of the tarts with the beaten egg white and pierce the dough three or four times down the center of the tart with a fork.

3. Preheat the air fryer to 350°F.

4. Air-fry the tarts in batches at 350°F for 6 minutes. Flip the tarts over and air-fry for an additional 3 minutes.

5. While the tarts are air-frying, make the icing. Combine the powdered sugar, ¼ cup strawberry preserves and milk in a bowl, whisking until the icing is smooth. Spread the icing over the top of each tart, leaving an empty border around the edges. Decorate with sprinkles if desired.

Gingerbread

Servings: 6

Cooking Time: 20 Minutes

Ingredients:

- cooking spray
- 1 cup flour
- 2 tablespoons sugar
- ¾ teaspoon ground ginger
- ¼ teaspoon cinnamon
- 1 teaspoon baking powder
- ½ teaspoon baking soda
- ⅛ teaspoon salt
- 1 egg
- ¼ cup molasses
- ½ cup buttermilk
- 2 tablespoons oil
- 1 teaspoon pure vanilla extract

Directions:

1. Preheat air fryer to 330°F.

2. Spray 6 x 6-inch baking dish lightly with cooking spray.

3. In a medium bowl, mix together all the dry ingredients.

4. In a separate bowl, beat the egg. Add molasses, buttermilk, oil, and vanilla and stir until well mixed.

5. Pour liquid mixture into dry ingredients and stir until well blended.

6. Pour batter into baking dish and cook at 330°F for 20minutes or until toothpick inserted in center of loaf comes out clean.

Orange Gooey Butter Cake

Servings: 6
Cooking Time: 85 Minutes

Ingredients:

- Crust Layer:
- ½ cup flour
- ¼ cup sugar
- ½ teaspoon baking powder
- ⅛ teaspoon salt
- 2 ounces (½ stick) unsalted European style butter, melted
- 1 egg
- 1 teaspoon orange extract
- 2 tablespoons orange zest
- Gooey Butter Layer:
- 8 ounces cream cheese, softened
- 4 ounces (1 stick) unsalted European style butter, melted
- 2 eggs
- 2 teaspoons orange extract
- 2 tablespoons orange zest
- 4 cups powdered sugar
- Garnish:
- powdered sugar
- orange slices

Directions:

1. Preheat the air fryer to 350°F.

2. Grease a 7-inch cake pan and line the bottom with parchment paper. Combine the flour, sugar, baking powder and salt in a bowl. Add the melted butter, egg, orange extract and orange zest. Mix well and press this mixture into the bottom of the greased cake pan. Lower the pan into the basket using an aluminum foil sling (fold a piece of aluminum foil into a strip about 2-inches wide by 24-inches long). Fold the ends of the aluminum foil over the top of the dish before returning the basket to the air fryer. Air-fry uncovered for 8 minutes.

3. To make the gooey butter layer, beat the cream cheese, melted butter, eggs, orange extract and orange zest in a large bowl using an electric hand mixer. Add the powdered sugar in stages, beat until smooth with each addition. Pour this mixture on top of the baked crust in the cake pan. Wrap the pan with a piece of greased aluminum foil, tenting the top of the foil to leave a little room for the cake to rise.

4. Air-fry for 60 minutes at 350°F. Remove the aluminum foil and air-fry for an additional 17 minutes.

5. Let the cake cool inside the pan for at least 10 minutes. Then, run a butter knife around the cake and let the cake cool completely in the pan. When cooled, run the butter knife around the edges of the cake again and invert it onto a plate and then back onto a serving platter. Sprinkle the powdered sugar over the top of the cake and garnish with orange slices.

Oreo-coated Peanut Butter Cups

Servings:8

Cooking Time: 4 Minutes

Ingredients:

- 8 Standard ¾-ounce peanut butter cups, frozen
- ⅓ cup All-purpose flour
- 2 Large egg white(s), beaten until foamy
- 16 Oreos or other creme-filled chocolate sandwich cookies, ground to crumbs in a food processor
- Vegetable oil spray

Directions:

1. Set up and fill three shallow soup plates or small pie plates on your counter: one for the flour, one for the beaten egg white(s), and one for the cookie crumbs.

2. Dip a frozen peanut butter cup in the flour, turning it to coat all sides. Shake off any excess, then set it in the beaten egg white(s). Turn it to coat all sides, then let any excess egg white slip back into the rest. Set the candy bar in the cookie crumbs. Turn to coat on all parts, even the sides. Dip the peanut butter cup back in the egg white(s) as before, then into the cookie crumbs as before, making sure you have a solid, even coating all around the cup. Set aside while you dip and coat the remaining cups.

3. When all the peanut butter cups are dipped and coated, lightly coat them on all sides with the vegetable oil spray. Set them on a plate and freeze while the air fryer heats.

4. Preheat the air fryer to 400°F.

5. Set the dipped cups wider side up in the basket with as much air space between them as possible. Air-fry undisturbed for 4 minutes, or until they feel soft but the coating is set.

6. Turn off the machine and remove the basket from it. Set aside the basket with the fried cups for 10 minutes. Use a nonstick-safe spatula to transfer the fried cups to a wire rack. Cool for at least another 5 minutes before serving.

Coconut-custard Pie

Servings: 4

Cooking Time: 20 Minutes

Ingredients:

- 1 cup milk
- ¼ cup plus 2 tablespoons sugar
- ¼ cup biscuit baking mix
- 1 teaspoon vanilla
- 2 eggs
- 2 tablespoons melted butter
- cooking spray
- ½ cup shredded, sweetened coconut

Directions:

1. Place all ingredients except coconut in a medium bowl.

2. Using a hand mixer, beat on high speed for 3minutes.

3. Let sit for 5minutes.

4. Preheat air fryer to 330°F.

5. Spray a 6-inch round or 6 x 6-inch square baking pan with cooking spray and place pan in air fryer basket.

6. Pour filling into pan and sprinkle coconut over top.

7. Cook pie at 330°F for 20 minutes or until center sets.

Coconut Macaroons

Servings: 12

Cooking Time: 8 Minutes

Ingredients:

- 1⅓ cups shredded, sweetened coconut
- 4½ teaspoons flour
- 2 tablespoons sugar
- 1 egg white
- ½ teaspoon almond extract

Directions:

1. Preheat air fryer to 330°F.
2. Mix all ingredients together.
3. Shape coconut mixture into 12 balls.
4. Place all 12 macaroons in air fryer basket. They won't expand, so you can place them close together, but they shouldn't touch.
5. Cook at 330°F for 8 minutes, until golden.

Blueberry Crisp

Servings: 6

Cooking Time: 13 Minutes

Ingredients:

- 3 cups Fresh or thawed frozen blueberries
- ⅓ cup Granulated white sugar
- 1 tablespoon Instant tapioca
- ⅓ cup All-purpose flour
- ⅓ cup Rolled oats (not quick-cooking or steel-cut)
- ⅓ cup Chopped walnuts or pecans
- ⅓ cup Packed light brown sugar
- 5 tablespoons plus 1 teaspoon (⅔ stick) Butter, melted and cooled
- ¾ teaspoon Ground cinnamon
- ¼ teaspoon Table salt

Directions:

1. Preheat the air fryer to 400°F.

2. Mix the blueberries, granulated white sugar, and instant tapioca in a 6-inch round cake pan for a small batch, a 7-inch round cake pan for a medium batch, or an 8-inch round cake pan for a large batch.

3. When the machine is at temperature, set the cake pan in the basket and air-fry undisturbed for 5 minutes, or just until the blueberries begin to bubble.

4. Meanwhile, mix the flour, oats, nuts, brown sugar, butter, cinnamon, and salt in a medium bowl until well combined.

5. When the blueberries have begun to bubble, crumble this flour mixture evenly on top. Continue air-frying undisturbed for 8 minutes, or until the topping has browned a bit and the filling is bubbling.

6. Use two hot pads or silicone baking mitts to transfer the cake pan to a wire rack. Cool for at least 10 minutes or to room temperature before serving.

Molten Chocolate Almond Cakes

Servings: 3

Cooking Time: 13 Minutes

Ingredients:

- butter and flour for the ramekins
- 4 ounces bittersweet chocolate, chopped
- ½ cup (1 stick) unsalted butter
- 2 eggs
- 2 egg yolks
- ¼ cup sugar
- ½ teaspoon pure vanilla extract, or almond extract
- 1 tablespoon all-purpose flour
- 3 tablespoons ground almonds

- 8 to 12 semisweet chocolate discs (or 4 chunks of chocolate)
- cocoa powder or powdered sugar, for dusting
- toasted almonds, coarsely chopped

Directions:

1. Butter and flour three (6-ounce) ramekins. (Butter the ramekins and then coat the butter with flour by shaking it around in the ramekin and dumping out any excess.)
2. Melt the chocolate and butter together, either in the microwave or in a double boiler. In a separate bowl, beat the eggs, egg yolks and sugar together until light and smooth. Add the vanilla extract. Whisk the chocolate mixture into the egg mixture. Stir in the flour and ground almonds.
3. Preheat the air fryer to 330°F.
4. Transfer the batter carefully to the buttered ramekins, filling halfway. Place two or three chocolate discs in the center of the batter and then fill the ramekins to ½-inch below the top with the remaining batter. Place the ramekins into the air fryer basket and air-fry at 330°F for 13 minutes. The sides of the cake should be set, but the centers should be slightly soft. Remove the ramekins from the air fryer and let the cakes sit for 5 minutes. (If you'd like the cake a little less molten, air-fry for 14 minutes and let the cakes sit for 4 minutes.)
5. Run a butter knife around the edge of the ramekins and invert the cakes onto a plate. Lift the ramekin off the plate slowly and carefully so that the cake doesn't break. Dust with cocoa powder or powdered sugar and serve with a scoop of ice cream and some coarsely chopped toasted almonds.

Chocolate Macaroons

Servings: 16
Cooking Time: 8 Minutes

Ingredients:

- 2 Large egg white(s), at room temperature
- ⅛ teaspoon Table salt
- ½ cup Granulated white sugar
- 1½ cups Unsweetened shredded coconut
- 3 tablespoons Unsweetened cocoa powder

Directions:

1. Preheat the air fryer to 375°F .
2. Using an electric mixer at high speed, beat the egg white(s) and salt in a medium or large bowl until stiff peaks can be formed when the turned-off beaters are dipped into the mixture.
3. Still working with the mixer at high speed, beat in the sugar in a slow stream until the meringue is shiny and thick.
4. Scrape down and remove the beaters. Fold in the coconut and cocoa with a rubber spatula until well combined, working carefully to deflate the meringue as little as possible.
5. Scoop up 2 tablespoons of the mixture. Wet your clean hands and roll that little bit of coconut bliss into a ball. Set it aside and continue making more balls: 7 more for a small batch, 15 more for a medium batch, or 23 more for a large one.
6. Line the bottom of the machine's basket or the basket attachment with parchment paper. Set the balls on the parchment with as much air space between them as possible. Air-fry undisturbed for 8 minutes, or until dry, set, and lightly browned.
7. Use a nonstick-safe spatula to transfer the macaroons to a wire rack. Cool for at least 10 minutes before serving. Or cool to room temperature, about 30 minutes, then store in a

sealed container at room temperature for up to 3 days.

Apple Crisp

Servings: 4
Cooking Time: 16 Minutes

Ingredients:
- Filling
- 3 Granny Smith apples, thinly sliced (about 4 cups)
- ¼ teaspoon ground cinnamon
- ⅛ teaspoon salt
- 1½ teaspoons lemon juice
- 2 tablespoons honey
- 1 tablespoon brown sugar
- cooking spray
- Crumb Topping
- 2 tablespoons oats
- 2 tablespoons oat bran
- 2 tablespoons cooked quinoa
- 2 tablespoons chopped walnuts
- 2 tablespoons brown sugar
- 2 teaspoons coconut oil

Directions:
1. Combine all filling ingredients and stir well so that apples are evenly coated.
2. Spray air fryer baking pan with nonstick cooking spray and spoon in the apple mixture.
3. Cook at 360°F for 5minutes. Stir well, scooping up from the bottom to mix apples and sauce.
4. At this point, the apples should be crisp-tender. Continue cooking in 3-minute intervals until apples are as soft as you like.
5. While apples are cooking, combine all topping ingredients in a small bowl. Stir until coconut oil mixes in well and distributes evenly. If your coconut oil is cold, it may be easier to mix in by hand.
6. When apples are cooked to your liking, sprinkle crumb mixture on top. Cook at 360°F for 8 minutes or until crumb topping is golden brown and crispy.

Chocolate Soufflés

Servings: 2
Cooking Time: 14 Minutes

Ingredients:
- butter and sugar for greasing the ramekins
- 3 ounces semi-sweet chocolate, chopped
- ¼ cup unsalted butter
- 2 eggs, yolks and white separated
- 3 tablespoons sugar
- ½ teaspoon pure vanilla extract
- 2 tablespoons all-purpose flour
- powdered sugar, for dusting the finished soufflés
- heavy cream, for serving

Directions:
1. Butter and sugar two 6-ounce ramekins. (Butter the ramekins and then coat the butter with sugar by shaking it around in the ramekin and dumping out any excess.)
2. Melt the chocolate and butter together, either in the microwave or in a double boiler. In a separate bowl, beat the egg yolks vigorously. Add the sugar and the vanilla extract and beat well again. Drizzle in the chocolate and butter, mixing well. Stir in the flour, combining until there are no lumps.
3. Preheat the air fryer to 330°F.
4. In a separate bowl, whisk the egg whites to soft peak stage (the point at which the whites can almost stand up on the end of your whisk). Fold

the whipped egg whites into the chocolate mixture gently and in stages.

5. Transfer the batter carefully to the buttered ramekins, leaving about ½-inch at the top. (You may have a little extra batter, depending on how airy the batter is, so you might be able to squeeze out a third soufflé if you want to.) Place the ramekins into the air fryer basket and air-fry for 14 minutes. The soufflés should have risen nicely and be brown on top. (Don't worry if the top gets a little dark – you'll be covering it with powdered sugar in the next step.)

6. Dust with powdered sugar and serve immediately with heavy cream to pour over the top at the table.

Hasselback Apple Crisp

Servings: 4

Cooking Time: 20 Minutes

Ingredients:

- 2 large Gala apples, peeled, cored and cut in half
- ¼ cup butter, melted
- ½ teaspoon ground cinnamon
- 2 tablespoons sugar
- Topping
- 3 tablespoons butter, melted
- 2 tablespoons brown sugar
- ¼ cup chopped pecans
- 2 tablespoons rolled oats*
- 1 tablespoon flour*
- vanilla ice cream
- caramel sauce

Directions:

1. Place the apples cut side down on a cutting board. Slicing from stem end to blossom end, make 8 to 10 slits down the apple halves but only slice three quarters of the way through the apple, not all the way through to the cutting board.

2. Preheat the air fryer to 330°F and pour a little water into the bottom of the air fryer drawer. (This will help prevent the grease that drips into the bottom drawer from burning and smoking.)

3. Transfer the apples to the air fryer basket, flat side down. Combine ¼ cup of melted butter, cinnamon and sugar in a small bowl. Brush this butter mixture onto the apples and air-fry at 330°F for 15 minutes. Baste the apples several times with the butter mixture during the cooking process.

4. While the apples are air-frying, make the filling. Combine 3 tablespoons of melted butter with the brown sugar, pecans, rolled oats and flour in a bowl. Stir with a fork until the mixture resembles small crumbles.

5. When the timer on the air fryer is up, spoon the topping down the center of the apples. Air-fry at 330°F for an additional 5 minutes.

6. Transfer the apples to a serving plate and serve with vanilla ice cream and caramel sauce.

Bananas Foster Bread Pudding

Servings: 4

Cooking Time: 25 Minutes

Ingredients:

- ½ cup brown sugar
- 3 eggs
- ¾ cup half and half
- 1 teaspoon pure vanilla extract
- 6 cups cubed Kings Hawaiian bread (½-inch cubes), ½ pound
- 2 bananas, sliced
- 1 cup caramel sauce, plus more for serving

Directions:

1. Preheat the air fryer to 350°F.

2. Combine the brown sugar, eggs, half and half and vanilla extract in a large bowl, whisking until the sugar has dissolved and the mixture is smooth. Stir in the cubed bread and toss to coat all the cubes evenly. Let the bread sit for 10 minutes to absorb the liquid.

3. Mix the sliced bananas and caramel sauce together in a separate bowl.

4. Fill the bottom of 4 (8-ounce) greased ramekins with half the bread cubes. Divide the caramel and bananas between the ramekins, spooning them on top of the bread cubes. Top with the remaining bread cubes and wrap each ramekin with aluminum foil, tenting the foil at the top to leave some room for the bread to puff up during the cooking process.

5. Air-fry two bread puddings at a time for 25 minutes. Let the puddings cool a little and serve warm with additional caramel sauce drizzled on top. A scoop of vanilla ice cream would be nice too and in keeping with our Bananas Foster theme!

Giant Buttery Chocolate Chip Cookie

Servings: 4

Cooking Time: 16 Minutes

Ingredients:

- ⅔ cup plus 1 tablespoon All-purpose flour
- ¼ teaspoon Baking soda
- ¼ teaspoon Table salt
- Baking spray (see the headnote)
- 4 tablespoons (¼ cup/½ stick) plus 1 teaspoon Butter, at room temperature
- ¼ cup plus 1 teaspoon Packed dark brown sugar
- 3 tablespoons plus 1 teaspoon Granulated white sugar
- 2½ tablespoons Pasteurized egg substitute, such as Egg Beaters
- ½ teaspoon Vanilla extract
- ¾ cup plus 1 tablespoon Semisweet or bittersweet chocolate chips

Directions:

1. Preheat the air fryer to 350°F .

2. Whisk the flour, baking soda, and salt in a bowl until well combined.

3. For a small air fryer, coat the inside of a 6-inch round cake pan with baking spray. For a medium air fryer, coat the inside of a 7-inch round cake pan with baking spray. And for a large air fryer, coat the inside of an 8-inch round cake pan with baking spray.

4. Using a hand electric mixer at medium speed, beat the butter, brown sugar, and granulated white sugar in a bowl until smooth and thick, about 3 minutes, scraping down the inside of the bowl several times.

5. Beat in the pasteurized egg substitute or egg (as applicable) and vanilla until uniform. Scrape down and remove the beaters. Fold in the flour mixture and chocolate chips with a rubber spatula, just until combined. Scrape and gently press this dough into the prepared pan, getting it even across the pan to the perimeter.

6. Set the pan in the basket and air-fry undisturbed for 16 minutes, or until the cookie is puffed, browned, and feels set to the touch.

7. Transfer the pan to a wire rack and cool for 10 minutes. Loosen the cookie from the perimeter with a spatula, then invert the pan onto a cutting board and let the cookie come free. Remove the pan and reinvert the cookie onto the

wire rack. Cool for 5 minutes more before slicing into wedges to serve.

Banana Bread Cake

Servings: 6
Cooking Time: 18-22 Minutes

Ingredients:

- ¾ cup plus 2 tablespoons All-purpose flour
- ½ teaspoon Baking powder
- ¼ teaspoon Baking soda
- ¼ teaspoon Table salt
- 4 tablespoons (¼ cup/½ stick) Butter, at room temperature
- ½ cup Granulated white sugar
- 2 Small ripe bananas, peeled
- 5 tablespoons Pasteurized egg substitute, such as Egg Beaters
- ¼ cup Buttermilk
- ¾ teaspoon Vanilla extract
- Baking spray (see here)

Directions:

1. Preheat the air fryer to 325°F (or 330°F, if that's the closest setting).
2. Mix the flour, baking powder, baking soda, and salt in a small bowl until well combined.
3. Using an electric hand mixer at medium speed, beat the butter and sugar in a medium bowl until creamy and smooth, about 3 minutes, occasionally scraping down the inside of the bowl.
4. Beat in the bananas until smooth. Then beat in egg substitute or egg, buttermilk, and vanilla until uniform. (The batter may look curdled at this stage. The flour mixture will smooth it out.) Add the flour mixture and beat at low speed until smooth and creamy.
5. Use the baking spray to generously coat the inside of a 6-inch round cake pan for a small batch, a 7-inch round cake pan for a medium batch, or an 8-inch round cake pan for a large batch. Scrape and spread the batter into the pan, smoothing the batter out to an even layer.
6. Set the pan in the basket and air-fry for 18 minutes for a 6-inch layer, 20 minutes for a 7-inch layer, or 22 minutes for an 8-inch layer, or until the cake is well browned and set even if there's a little soft give right at the center. Start checking it at the 16-minute mark to know where you are.
7. Use hot pads or silicone baking mitts to transfer the cake pan to a wire rack. To unmold, set a cutting board over the baking pan and invert both the board and the pan. Lift the still-warm pan off the cake layer. Set the wire rack on top of that layer and invert all of it with the cutting board so that the cake layer is now right side up on the wire rack. Remove the cutting board and continue cooling the cake for at least 10 minutes or to room temperature, about 40 minutes, before slicing into wedges.

Honey-pecan Yogurt Cake

Servings: 6
Cooking Time: 18-24 Minutes

Ingredients:

- 1 cup plus 3½ tablespoons All-purpose flour
- ¼ teaspoon Baking powder
- ¼ teaspoon Baking soda
- ¼ teaspoon Table salt
- 5 tablespoons Plain full-fat, low-fat, or fat-free Greek yogurt
- 5 tablespoons Honey
- 5 tablespoons Pasteurized egg substitute, such as Egg Beaters
- 2 teaspoons Vanilla extract

* ⅔ cup Chopped pecans
* Baking spray (see here)

Directions:

1. Preheat the air fryer to 325°F (or 330°F, if the closest setting).
2. Mix the flour, baking powder, baking soda, and salt in a small bowl until well combined.
3. Using an electric hand mixer at medium speed , beat the yogurt, honey, egg substitute or egg, and vanilla in a medium bowl until smooth, about 2 minutes, scraping down the inside of the bowl once or twice.
4. Turn off the mixer; scrape down and remove the beaters. Fold in the flour mixture with a rubber spatula, just until all of the flour has been moistened. Fold in the pecans until they are evenly distributed in the mixture.
5. Use the baking spray to generously coat the inside of a 6-inch round cake pan for a small batch, a 7-inch round cake pan for a medium batch, or an 8-inch round cake pan for a large batch. Scrape and spread the batter into the pan, smoothing the batter out to an even layer.
6. Set the pan in the basket and air-fry for 18 minutes for a 6-inch layer, 22 minutes for a 7-inch layer, or 24 minutes for an 8-inch layer, or until a toothpick or cake tester inserted into the center of the cake comes out clean. Start checking it at the 15-minute mark to know where you are.
7. Use hot pads or silicone baking mitts to transfer the cake pan to a wire rack. Cool for 5 minutes. To unmold, set a cutting board over the baking pan and invert both the board and the pan. Lift the still-warm pan off the cake layer. Set the wire rack on top of that layer and invert all of it with the cutting board so that the cake layer is now right side up on the wire rack. Remove the cutting board and continue cooling the cake for at least 10 minutes or to room temperature, about 30 minutes, before slicing into wedges.

Sugared Pizza Dough Dippers With Raspberry Cream Cheese Dip

Servings: 10
Cooking Time: 8 Minutes

Ingredients:
* 1 pound pizza dough*
* ½ cup butter, melted
* ¾ to 1 cup sugar
* Raspberry Cream Cheese Dip
* 4 ounces cream cheese, softened
* 2 tablespoons powdered sugar
* ½ teaspoon almond extract or almond paste
* 1½ tablespoons milk
* ¼ cup raspberry preserves
* fresh raspberries

Directions:

1. Cut the ingredients in half or save half of the dough for another recipe.
2. When you're ready to make your sugared dough dippers, remove your pizza dough from the refrigerator at least 1 hour prior to baking and let it sit on the counter, covered gently with plastic wrap.
3. Roll the dough into two 15-inch logs. Cut each log into 20 slices and roll each slice so that it is 3- to 3½-inches long. Cut each slice in half and twist the dough halves together 3 to 4 times. Place the twisted dough on a cookie sheet, brush with melted butter and sprinkle sugar over the dough twists.
4. Preheat the air fryer to 350°F.
5. Brush the bottom of the air fryer basket with a little melted butter. Air-fry the dough twists in

batches. Place 8 to 12 (depending on the size of your air fryer) in the air fryer basket.

6. Air-fry for 6 minutes. Turn the dough strips over and brush the other side with butter. Air-fry for an additional 2 minutes.

7. While the dough twists are cooking, make the cream cheese and raspberry dip. Whip the cream cheese with a hand mixer until fluffy. Add the powdered sugar, almond extract and milk, and beat until smooth. Fold in the raspberry preserves and transfer to a serving dish.

8. As the batches of dough twists are complete, place them into a shallow dish. Brush with more melted butter and generously coat with sugar, shaking the dish to cover both sides. Serve the sugared dough dippers warm with the raspberry cream cheese dip on the side. Garnish with fresh raspberries.

Peach Cobbler

Servings: 4
Cooking Time: 12 Minutes

Ingredients:

- 16 ounces frozen peaches, thawed, with juice (do not drain)
- 6 tablespoons sugar
- 1 tablespoon cornstarch
- 1 tablespoon water
- Crust
- ½ cup flour
- ¼ teaspoon salt
- 3 tablespoons butter
- 1½ tablespoons cold water
- ¼ teaspoon sugar

Directions:

1. Place peaches, including juice, and sugar in air fryer baking pan. Stir to mix well.

2. In a small cup, dissolve cornstarch in the water. Stir into peaches.

3. In a medium bowl, combine the flour and salt. Cut in butter using knives or a pastry blender. Stir in the cold water to make a stiff dough.

4. On a floured board or wax paper, pat dough into a square or circle slightly smaller than your air fryer baking pan. Cut diagonally into 4 pieces.

5. Place dough pieces on top of peaches, leaving a tiny bit of space between the edges. Sprinkle very lightly with sugar, no more than about ¼ teaspoon.

6. Cook at 360°F for 12 minutes, until fruit bubbles and crust browns.

Fried Banana S'mores

Servings: 4
Cooking Time: 6 Minutes

Ingredients:

- 4 bananas
- 3 tablespoons mini semi-sweet chocolate chips
- 3 tablespoons mini peanut butter chips
- 3 tablespoons mini marshmallows
- 3 tablespoons graham cracker cereal

Directions:

1. Preheat the air fryer to 400°F.

2. Slice into the un-peeled bananas lengthwise along the inside of the curve, but do not slice through the bottom of the peel. Open the banana slightly to form a pocket.

3. Fill each pocket with chocolate chips, peanut butter chips and marshmallows. Poke the graham cracker cereal into the filling.

4. Place the bananas in the air fryer basket, resting them on the side of the basket and each other to keep them upright with the filling facing

up. Air-fry for 6 minutes, or until the bananas are soft to the touch, the peels have blackened and the chocolate and marshmallows have melted and toasted.

5. Let them cool for a couple of minutes and then simply serve with a spoon to scoop out the filling.

Brown Sugar Baked Apples

Servings: 4

Cooking Time: 15 Minutes

Ingredients:

- 3 Small tart apples, preferably McIntosh
- 4 tablespoons (¼ cup/½ stick) Butter
- 6 tablespoons Light brown sugar
- Ground cinnamon
- Table salt

Directions:

1. Preheat the air fryer to 400°F.
2. Stem the apples, then cut them in half through their "equators" (that is, not the stem ends). Use a melon baller to core the apples, taking care not to break through the flesh and skin at any point but creating a little well in the center of each half.

3. When the machine is at temperature, remove the basket and set it on a heat-safe work surface. Set the apple halves cut side up in the basket with as much air space between them as possible. Even a fraction of an inch will work. Drop 2 teaspoons of butter into the well in the center of each apple half. Sprinkle each half with 1 tablespoon brown sugar and a pinch each ground cinnamon and table salt.

4. Return the basket to the machine. Air-fry undisturbed for 15 minutes, or until the apple halves have softened and the brown sugar has caramelized.

5. Use a nonstick-safe spatula to transfer the apple halves cut side up to a wire rack. Cool for at least 10 minutes before serving, or serve at room temperature.

Sandwiches And Burgers Recipes

Mexican Cheeseburgers

Servings: 4
Cooking Time: 22 Minutes

Ingredients:

- 1¼ pounds ground beef
- ¼ cup finely chopped onion
- ½ cup crushed yellow corn tortilla chips
- 1 (1.25-ounce) packet taco seasoning
- ¼ cup canned diced green chilies
- 1 egg, lightly beaten
- 4 ounces pepper jack cheese, grated
- 4 (12-inch) flour tortillas
- shredded lettuce, sour cream, guacamole, salsa (for topping)

Directions:

1. Combine the ground beef, minced onion, crushed tortilla chips, taco seasoning, green chilies, and egg in a large bowl. Mix thoroughly until combined – your hands are good tools for this. Divide the meat into four equal portions and shape each portion into an oval-shaped burger.
2. Preheat the air fryer to 370°F.
3. Air-fry the burgers for 18 minutes, turning them over halfway through the cooking time. Divide the cheese between the burgers, lower fryer to 340°F and air-fry for an additional 4 minutes to melt the cheese. (This will give you a burger that is medium-well. If you prefer your cheeseburger medium-rare, shorten the cooking time to about 15 minutes and then add the cheese and proceed with the recipe.)
4. While the burgers are cooking, warm the tortillas wrapped in aluminum foil in a 350°F oven, or in a skillet with a little oil over medium-high heat for a couple of minutes. Keep the tortillas warm until the burgers are ready.
5. To assemble the burgers, spread sour cream over three quarters of the tortillas and top each with some shredded lettuce and salsa. Place the Mexican cheeseburgers on the lettuce and top with guacamole. Fold the tortillas around the burger, starting with the bottom and then folding the sides in over the top. (A little sour cream can help hold the seam of the tortilla together.) Serve immediately.

Inside-out Cheeseburgers

Servings: 3
Cooking Time: 9-11 Minutes

Ingredients:

- 1 pound 2 ounces 90% lean ground beef
- ¾ teaspoon Dried oregano
- ¾ teaspoon Table salt
- ¾ teaspoon Ground black pepper
- ¼ teaspoon Garlic powder
- 6 tablespoons (about 1½ ounces) Shredded Cheddar, Swiss, or other semi-firm cheese, or a purchased blend of shredded cheeses
- 3 Hamburger buns (gluten-free, if a concern), split open

Directions:

1. Preheat the air fryer to 375°F .
2. Gently mix the ground beef, oregano, salt, pepper, and garlic powder in a bowl until well combined without turning the mixture to mush. Form it into two 6-inch patties for the small batch, three for the medium, or four for the large.
3. Place 2 tablespoons of the shredded cheese in the center of each patty. With clean hands, fold

the sides of the patty up to cover the cheese, then pick it up and roll it gently into a ball to seal the cheese inside. Gently press it back into a 5-inch burger without letting any cheese squish out. Continue filling and preparing more burgers, as needed.

4. Place the burgers in the basket in one layer and air-fry undisturbed for 8 minutes for medium or 10 minutes for well-done. (An instant-read meat thermometer won't work for these burgers because it will hit the mostly melted cheese inside and offer a hotter temperature than the surrounding meat.)

5. Use a nonstick-safe spatula, and perhaps a flatware fork for balance, to transfer the burgers to a cutting board. Set the buns cut side down in the basket in one layer (working in batches as necessary) and air-fry undisturbed for 1 minute, to toast a bit and warm up. Cool the burgers a few minutes more, then serve them warm in the buns.

Reuben Sandwiches

Servings: 2

Cooking Time: 11 Minutes

Ingredients:

- ½ pound Sliced deli corned beef
- 4 teaspoons Regular or low-fat mayonnaise (not fat-free)
- 4 Rye bread slices
- 2 tablespoons plus 2 teaspoons Russian dressing
- ½ cup Purchased sauerkraut, squeezed by the handful over the sink to get rid of excess moisture
- 2 ounces (2 to 4 slices) Swiss cheese slices (optional)

Directions:

1. Set the corned beef in the basket, slip the basket into the machine, and heat the air fryer to 400°F. Air-fry undisturbed for 3 minutes from the time the basket is put in the machine, just to warm up the meat.

2. Use kitchen tongs to transfer the corned beef to a cutting board. Spread 1 teaspoon mayonnaise on one side of each slice of rye bread, rubbing the mayonnaise into the bread with a small flatware knife.

3. Place the bread slices mayonnaise side down on a cutting board. Spread the Russian dressing over the "dry" side of each slice. For one sandwich, top one slice of bread with the corned beef, sauerkraut, and cheese (if using). For two sandwiches, top two slices of bread each with half of the corned beef, sauerkraut, and cheese (if using). Close the sandwiches with the remaining bread, setting it mayonnaise side up on top.

4. Set the sandwich(es) in the basket and air-fry undisturbed for 8 minutes, or until browned and crunchy.

5. Use a nonstick-safe spatula, and perhaps a flatware fork for balance, to transfer the sandwich(es) to a cutting board. Cool for 2 or 3 minutes before slicing in half and serving.

Chicken Spiedies

Servings: 3

Cooking Time: 12 Minutes

Ingredients:

- 1¼ pounds Boneless skinless chicken thighs, trimmed of any fat blobs and cut into 2-inch pieces
- 3 tablespoons Red wine vinegar
- 2 tablespoons Olive oil
- 2 tablespoons Minced fresh mint leaves

- 2 tablespoons Minced fresh parsley leaves
- 2 teaspoons Minced fresh dill fronds
- ¾ teaspoon Fennel seeds
- ¾ teaspoon Table salt
- Up to a ¼ teaspoon Red pepper flakes
- 3 Long soft rolls, such as hero, hoagie, or Italian sub rolls (gluten-free, if a concern), split open lengthwise
- 4½ tablespoons Regular or low-fat mayonnaise (not fat-free; gluten-free, if a concern)
- 1½ tablespoons Distilled white vinegar
- 1½ teaspoons Ground black pepper

Directions:

1. Mix the chicken, vinegar, oil, mint, parsley, dill, fennel seeds, salt, and red pepper flakes in a zip-closed plastic bag. Seal, gently massage the marinade ingredients into the meat, and refrigerate for at least 2 hours or up to 6 hours. (Longer than that and the meat can turn rubbery.)

2. Set the plastic bag out on the counter (to make the contents a little less frigid). Preheat the air fryer to 400°F.

3. When the machine is at temperature, use kitchen tongs to set the chicken thighs in the basket (discard any remaining marinade) and air-fry undisturbed for 6 minutes. Turn the thighs over and continue air-frying undisturbed for 6 minutes more, until well browned, cooked through, and even a little crunchy.

4. Dump the contents of the basket onto a wire rack and cool for 2 or 3 minutes. Divide the chicken evenly between the rolls. Whisk the mayonnaise, vinegar, and black pepper in a small bowl until smooth. Drizzle this sauce over the chicken pieces in the rolls.

White Bean Veggie Burgers

Servings: 3
Cooking Time: 13 Minutes

Ingredients:

- 1⅓ cups Drained and rinsed canned white beans
- 3 tablespoons Rolled oats (not quick-cooking or steel-cut; gluten-free, if a concern)
- 3 tablespoons Chopped walnuts
- 2 teaspoons Olive oil
- 2 teaspoons Lemon juice
- 1½ teaspoons Dijon mustard (gluten-free, if a concern)
- ¾ teaspoon Dried sage leaves
- ¼ teaspoon Table salt
- Olive oil spray
- 3 Whole-wheat buns or gluten-free whole-grain buns (if a concern), split open

Directions:

1. Preheat the air fryer to 400°F.

2. Place the beans, oats, walnuts, oil, lemon juice, mustard, sage, and salt in a food processor. Cover and process to make a coarse paste that will hold its shape, about like wet sugar-cookie dough, stopping the machine to scrape down the inside of the canister at least once.

3. Scrape down and remove the blade. With clean and wet hands, form the bean paste into two 4-inch patties for the small batch, three 4-inch patties for the medium, or four 4-inch patties for the large batch. Generously coat the patties on both sides with olive oil spray.

4. Set them in the basket with some space between them and air-fry undisturbed for 12 minutes, or until lightly brown and crisp at the edges. The tops of the burgers will feel firm to the touch.

5. Use a nonstick-safe spatula, and perhaps a flatware fork for balance, to transfer the burgers to a cutting board. Set the buns cut side down in the basket in one layer (working in batches as necessary) and air-fry undisturbed for 1 minute, to toast a bit and warm up. Serve the burgers warm in the buns.

Black Bean Veggie Burgers

Servings: 3
Cooking Time: 10 Minutes

Ingredients:

- 1 cup Drained and rinsed canned black beans
- ⅓ cup Pecan pieces
- ⅓ cup Rolled oats (not quick-cooking or steel-cut; gluten-free, if a concern)
- 2 tablespoons (or 1 small egg) Pasteurized egg substitute, such as Egg Beaters (gluten-free, if a concern)
- 2 teaspoons Red ketchup-like chili sauce, such as Heinz
- ¼ teaspoon Ground cumin
- ¼ teaspoon Dried oregano
- ¼ teaspoon Table salt
- ¼ teaspoon Ground black pepper
- Olive oil
- Olive oil spray

Directions:

1. Preheat the air fryer to 400°F.
2. Put the beans, pecans, oats, egg substitute or egg, chili sauce, cumin, oregano, salt, and pepper in a food processor. Cover and process to a coarse paste that will hold its shape like sugar-cookie dough, adding olive oil in 1-teaspoon increments to get the mixture to blend smoothly. The amount of olive oil is actually dependent on the internal moisture content of the beans and the oats. Figure on about 1 tablespoon (three 1-teaspoon additions) for the smaller batch, with proportional increases for the other batches. A little too much olive oil can't hurt, but a dry paste will fall apart as it cooks and a far-too-wet paste will stick to the basket.
3. Scrape down and remove the blade. Using clean, wet hands, form the paste into two 4-inch patties for the small batch, three 4-inch patties for the medium, or four 4-inch patties for the large batch, setting them one by one on a cutting board. Generously coat both sides of the patties with olive oil spray.
4. Set them in the basket in one layer. Air-fry undisturbed for 10 minutes, or until lightly browned and crisp at the edges.
5. Use a nonstick-safe spatula, and perhaps a flatware fork for balance, to transfer the burgers to a wire rack. Cool for 5 minutes before serving.

Turkey Burgers

Servings: 3
Cooking Time: 23 Minutes

Ingredients:

- 1 pound 2 ounces Ground turkey
- 6 tablespoons Frozen chopped spinach, thawed and squeezed dry
- 3 tablespoons Plain panko bread crumbs (gluten-free, if a concern)
- 1 tablespoon Dijon mustard (gluten-free, if a concern)
- 1½ teaspoons Minced garlic
- ¾ teaspoon Table salt
- ¾ teaspoon Ground black pepper
- Olive oil spray
- 3 Kaiser rolls (gluten-free, if a concern), split open

Directions:
1. Preheat the air fryer to 375°F .
2. Gently mix the ground turkey, spinach, bread crumbs, mustard, garlic, salt, and pepper in a large bowl until well combined, trying to keep some of the fibers of the ground turkey intact. Form into two 5-inch-wide patties for the small batch, three 5-inch patties for the medium batch, or four 5-inch patties for the large. Coat each side of the patties with olive oil spray.
3. Set the patties in in the basket in one layer and air-fry undisturbed for 20 minutes, or until an instant-read meat thermometer inserted into the center of a burger registers 165°F. You may need to add 2 minutes to the cooking time if the air fryer is at 360°F.
4. Use a nonstick-safe spatula, and perhaps a flatware fork for balance, to transfer the burgers to a cutting board. Set the buns cut side down in the basket in one layer (working in batches as necessary) and air-fry for 1 minute, to toast a bit and warm up. Serve the burgers warm in the buns.

Crunchy Falafel Balls

Servings: 8
Cooking Time: 16 Minutes

Ingredients:
*   2½ cups Drained and rinsed canned chickpeas
*   ¼ cup Olive oil
*   3 tablespoons All-purpose flour
*   1½ teaspoons Dried oregano
*   1½ teaspoons Dried sage leaves
*   1½ teaspoons Dried thyme
*   ¾ teaspoon Table salt
*   Olive oil spray

Directions:
1. Preheat the air fryer to 400°F.

2. Place the chickpeas, olive oil, flour, oregano, sage, thyme, and salt in a food processor. Cover and process into a paste, stopping the machine at least once to scrape down the inside of the canister.
3. Scrape down and remove the blade. Using clean, wet hands, form 2 tablespoons of the paste into a ball, then continue making 9 more balls for a small batch, 15 more for a medium one, and 19 more for a large batch. Generously coat the balls in olive oil spray.
4. Set the balls in the basket in one layer with a little space between them and air-fry undisturbed for 16 minutes, or until well browned and crisp.
5. Dump the contents of the basket onto a wire rack. Cool for 5 minutes before serving.

Thanksgiving Turkey Sandwiches

Servings: 3
Cooking Time: 10 Minutes

Ingredients:
*   1½ cups Herb-seasoned stuffing mix (not cornbread-style; gluten-free, if a concern)
*   1 Large egg white(s)
*   2 tablespoons Water
*   3 5- to 6-ounce turkey breast cutlets
*   Vegetable oil spray
*   4½ tablespoons Purchased cranberry sauce, preferably whole berry
*   ⅛ teaspoon Ground cinnamon
*   ⅛ teaspoon Ground dried ginger
*   4½ tablespoons Regular, low-fat, or fat-free mayonnaise (gluten-free, if a concern)
*   6 tablespoons Shredded Brussels sprouts
*   3 Kaiser rolls (gluten-free, if a concern), split open

Directions:

1. Preheat the air fryer to 375°F .
2. Put the stuffing mix in a heavy zip-closed bag, seal it, lay it flat on your counter, and roll a rolling pin over the bag to crush the stuffing mix to the consistency of rough sand. (Or you can pulse the stuffing mix to the desired consistency in a food processor.)
3. Set up and fill two shallow soup plates or small pie plates on your counter: one for the egg white(s), whisked with the water until foamy; and one for the ground stuffing mix.
4. Dip a cutlet in the egg white mixture, coating both sides and letting any excess egg white slip back into the rest. Set the cutlet in the ground stuffing mix and coat it evenly on both sides, pressing gently to coat well on both sides. Lightly coat the cutlet on both sides with vegetable oil spray, set it aside, and continue dipping and coating the remaining cutlets in the same way.
5. Set the cutlets in the basket and air-fry undisturbed for 10 minutes, or until crisp and brown. Use kitchen tongs to transfer the cutlets to a wire rack to cool for a few minutes.
6. Meanwhile, stir the cranberry sauce with the cinnamon and ginger in a small bowl. Mix the shredded Brussels sprouts and mayonnaise in a second bowl until the vegetable is evenly coated.
7. Build the sandwiches by spreading about 1½ tablespoons of the cranberry mixture on the cut side of the bottom half of each roll. Set a cutlet on top, then spread about 3 tablespoons of the Brussels sprouts mixture evenly over the cutlet. Set the other half of the roll on top and serve warm.

Thai-style Pork Sliders

Servings: 4

Cooking Time: 15 Minutes

Ingredients:
- 11 ounces Ground pork
- 2½ tablespoons Very thinly sliced scallions, white and green parts
- 4 teaspoons Minced peeled fresh ginger
- 2½ teaspoons Fish sauce (gluten-free, if a concern)
- 2 teaspoons Thai curry paste (see the headnote; gluten-free, if a concern)
- 2 teaspoons Light brown sugar
- ¾ teaspoon Ground black pepper
- 4 Slider buns (gluten-free, if a concern)

Directions:
1. Preheat the air fryer to 375°F .
2. Gently mix the pork, scallions, ginger, fish sauce, curry paste, brown sugar, and black pepper in a bowl until well combined. With clean, wet hands, form about ⅓ cup of the pork mixture into a slider about 2½ inches in diameter. Repeat until you use up all the meat—3 sliders for the small batch, 4 for the medium, and 6 for the large. (Keep wetting your hands to help the patties adhere.)
3. When the machine is at temperature, set the sliders in the basket in one layer. Air-fry undisturbed for 14 minutes, or until the sliders are golden brown and caramelized at their edges and an instant-read meat thermometer inserted into the center of a slider registers 160°F.
4. Use a nonstick-safe spatula, and perhaps a flatware fork for balance, to transfer the sliders to a cutting board. Set the buns cut side down in the basket in one layer (working in batches as necessary) and air-fry undisturbed for 1 minute, to toast a bit and warm up. Serve the sliders warm in the buns.

Inside Out Cheeseburgers

Servings: 2
Cooking Time: 20 Minutes

Ingredients:
- ¾ pound lean ground beef
- 3 tablespoons minced onion
- 4 teaspoons ketchup
- 2 teaspoons yellow mustard
- salt and freshly ground black pepper
- 4 slices of Cheddar cheese, broken into smaller pieces
- 8 hamburger dill pickle chips

Directions:
1. Combine the ground beef, minced onion, ketchup, mustard, salt and pepper in a large bowl. Mix well to thoroughly combine the ingredients. Divide the meat into four equal portions.
2. To make the stuffed burgers, flatten each portion of meat into a thin patty. Place 4 pickle chips and half of the cheese onto the center of two of the patties, leaving a rim around the edge of the patty exposed. Place the remaining two patties on top of the first and press the meat together firmly, sealing the edges tightly. With the burgers on a flat surface, press the sides of the burger with the palm of your hand to create a straight edge. This will help keep the stuffing inside the burger while it cooks.
3. Preheat the air fryer to 370°F.
4. Place the burgers inside the air fryer basket and air-fry for 20 minutes, flipping the burgers over halfway through the cooking time.
5. Serve the cheeseburgers on buns with lettuce and tomato.

Chicken Apple Brie Melt

Servings: 3
Cooking Time: 13 Minutes

Ingredients:
- 3 5- to 6-ounce boneless skinless chicken breasts
- Vegetable oil spray
- 1½ teaspoons Dried herbes de Provence
- 3 ounces Brie, rind removed, thinly sliced
- 6 Thin cored apple slices
- 3 French rolls (gluten-free, if a concern)
- 2 tablespoons Dijon mustard (gluten-free, if a concern)

Directions:
1. Preheat the air fryer to 375°F.
2. Lightly coat all sides of the chicken breasts with vegetable oil spray. Sprinkle the breasts evenly with the herbes de Provence.
3. When the machine is at temperature, set the breasts in the basket and air-fry undisturbed for 10 minutes.
4. Top the chicken breasts with the apple slices, then the cheese. Air-fry undisturbed for 2 minutes, or until the cheese is melty and bubbling.
5. Use a nonstick-safe spatula and kitchen tongs, for balance, to transfer the breasts to a cutting board. Set the rolls in the basket and air-fry for 1 minute to warm through. (Putting them in the machine without splitting them keeps the insides very soft while the outside gets a little crunchy.)
6. Transfer the rolls to the cutting board. Split them open lengthwise, then spread 1 teaspoon mustard on each cut side. Set a prepared chicken breast on the bottom of a roll and close with its top, repeating as necessary to make additional sandwiches. Serve warm.

Chicken Club Sandwiches

Servings: 3

Cooking Time: 15 Minutes

Ingredients:

- 3 5- to 6-ounce boneless skinless chicken breasts
- 6 Thick-cut bacon strips (gluten-free, if a concern)
- 3 Long soft rolls, such as hero, hoagie, or Italian sub rolls (gluten-free, if a concern)
- 3 tablespoons Regular, low-fat, or fat-free mayonnaise (gluten-free, if a concern)
- 3 Lettuce leaves, preferably romaine or iceberg
- 6 ¼-inch-thick tomato slices

Directions:

1. Preheat the air fryer to 375°F .

2. Wrap each chicken breast with 2 strips of bacon, spiraling the bacon around the meat, slightly overlapping the strips on each revolution. Start the second strip of bacon farther down the breast but on a line with the start of the first strip so they both end at a lined-up point on the chicken breast.

3. When the machine is at temperature, set the wrapped breasts bacon-seam side down in the basket with space between them. Air-fry undisturbed for 12 minutes, until the bacon is browned, crisp, and cooked through and an instant-read meat thermometer inserted into the center of a breast registers 165°F. You may need to add 2 minutes in the air fryer if the temperature is at 360°F.

4. Use kitchen tongs to transfer the breasts to a wire rack. Split the rolls open lengthwise and set them cut side down in the basket. Air-fry for 1 minute, or until warmed through.

5. Use kitchen tongs to transfer the rolls to a cutting board. Spread 1 tablespoon mayonnaise on the cut side of one half of each roll. Top with a chicken breast, lettuce leaf, and tomato slice. Serve warm.

Chili Cheese Dogs

Servings: 3
Cooking Time: 12 Minutes

Ingredients:

- ¾ pound Lean ground beef
- 1½ tablespoons Chile powder
- 1 cup plus 2 tablespoons Jarred sofrito
- 3 Hot dogs (gluten-free, if a concern)
- 3 Hot dog buns (gluten-free, if a concern), split open lengthwise
- 3 tablespoons Finely chopped scallion
- 9 tablespoons (a little more than 2 ounces) Shredded Cheddar cheese

Directions:

1. Crumble the ground beef into a medium or large saucepan set over medium heat. Brown well, stirring often to break up the clumps. Add the chile powder and cook for 30 seconds, stirring the whole time. Stir in the sofrito and bring to a simmer. Reduce the heat to low and simmer, stirring occasionally, for 5 minutes. Keep warm.

2. Preheat the air fryer to 400°F.

3. When the machine is at temperature, put the hot dogs in the basket and air-fry undisturbed for 10 minutes, or until the hot dogs are bubbling and blistered, even a little crisp.

4. Use kitchen tongs to put the hot dogs in the buns. Top each with a ½ cup of the ground beef mixture, 1 tablespoon of the minced scallion, and 3 tablespoons of the cheese. (The scallion should go under the cheese so it superheats and wilts a bit.) Set the filled hot dog buns in the basket and

air-fry undisturbed for 2 minutes, or until the cheese has melted.

5. Remove the basket from the machine. Cool the chili cheese dogs in the basket for 5 minutes before serving.

Dijon Thyme Burgers

Servings: 3
Cooking Time: 18 Minutes

Ingredients:

- 1 pound lean ground beef
- ⅓ cup panko breadcrumbs
- ¼ cup finely chopped onion
- 3 tablespoons Dijon mustard
- 1 tablespoon chopped fresh thyme
- 4 teaspoons Worcestershire sauce
- 1 teaspoon salt
- freshly ground black pepper
- Topping (optional):
- 2 tablespoons Dijon mustard
- 1 tablespoon dark brown sugar
- 1 teaspoon Worcestershire sauce
- 4 ounces sliced Swiss cheese, optional

Directions:

1. Combine all the burger ingredients together in a large bowl and mix well. Divide the meat into 4 equal portions and then form the burgers, being careful not to over-handle the meat. One good way to do this is to throw the meat back and forth from one hand to another, packing the meat each time you catch it. Flatten the balls into patties, making an indentation in the center of each patty with your thumb (this will help it stay flat as it cooks) and flattening the sides of the burgers so that they will fit nicely into the air fryer basket.

2. Preheat the air fryer to 370°F.

3. If you don't have room for all four burgers, air-fry two or three burgers at a time for 8 minutes. Flip the burgers over and air-fry for another 6 minutes.

4. While the burgers are cooking combine the Dijon mustard, dark brown sugar, and Worcestershire sauce in a small bowl and mix well. This optional topping to the burgers really adds a boost of flavor at the end. Spread the Dijon topping evenly on each burger. If you cooked the burgers in batches, return the first batch to the cooker at this time – it's ok to place the fourth burger on top of the others in the center of the basket. Air-fry the burgers for another 3 minutes.

5. Finally, if desired, top each burger with a slice of Swiss cheese. Lower the air fryer temperature to 330°F and air-fry for another minute to melt the cheese. Serve the burgers on toasted brioche buns, dressed the way you like them.

Provolone Stuffed Meatballs

Servings: 4
Cooking Time: 12 Minutes

Ingredients:

- 1 tablespoon olive oil
- 1 small onion, very finely chopped
- 1 to 2 cloves garlic, minced
- ¾ pound ground beef
- ¾ pound ground pork
- ¾ cup breadcrumbs
- ¼ cup grated Parmesan cheese
- ¼ cup finely chopped fresh parsley (or 1 tablespoon dried parsley)
- ½ teaspoon dried oregano
- 1½ teaspoons salt
- freshly ground black pepper

- 2 eggs, lightly beaten
- 5 ounces sharp or aged provolone cheese, cut into 1-inch cubes

Directions:
1. Preheat a skillet over medium-high heat. Add the oil and cook the onion and garlic until tender, but not browned.
2. Transfer the onion and garlic to a large bowl and add the beef, pork, breadcrumbs, Parmesan cheese, parsley, oregano, salt, pepper and eggs. Mix well until all the ingredients are combined. Divide the mixture into 12 evenly sized balls. Make one meatball at a time, by pressing a hole in the meatball mixture with your finger and pushing a piece of provolone cheese into the hole. Mold the meat back into a ball, enclosing the cheese.
3. Preheat the air fryer to 380°F.
4. Working in two batches, transfer six of the meatballs to the air fryer basket and air-fry for 12 minutes, shaking the basket and turning the meatballs a couple of times during the cooking process. Repeat with the remaining six meatballs. You can pop the first batch of meatballs into the air fryer for the last two minutes of cooking to re-heat them. Serve warm.

Philly Cheesesteak Sandwiches

Servings: 3
Cooking Time: 9 Minutes

Ingredients:
- ¾ pound Shaved beef
- 1 tablespoon Worcestershire sauce (gluten-free, if a concern)
- ¼ teaspoon Garlic powder
- ¼ teaspoon Mild paprika
- 6 tablespoons (1½ ounces) Frozen bell pepper strips (do not thaw)
- 2 slices, broken into rings Very thin yellow or white medium onion slice(s)
- 6 ounces (6 to 8 slices) Provolone cheese slices
- 3 Long soft rolls such as hero, hoagie, or Italian sub rolls, or hot dog buns (gluten-free, if a concern), split open lengthwise

Directions:
1. Preheat the air fryer to 400°F.
2. When the machine is at temperature, spread the shaved beef in the basket, leaving a ½-inch perimeter around the meat for good air flow. Sprinkle the meat with the Worcestershire sauce, paprika, and garlic powder. Spread the peppers and onions on top of the meat.
3. Air-fry undisturbed for 6 minutes, or until cooked through. Set the cheese on top of the meat. Continue air-frying undisturbed for 3 minutes, or until the cheese has melted.
4. Use kitchen tongs to divide the meat and cheese layers in the basket between the rolls or buns. Serve hot.

Eggplant Parmesan Subs

Servings: 2
Cooking Time: 13 Minutes

Ingredients:
- 4 Peeled eggplant slices (about ½ inch thick and 3 inches in diameter)
- Olive oil spray
- 2 tablespoons plus 2 teaspoons Jarred pizza sauce, any variety except creamy
- ¼ cup (about ⅔ ounce) Finely grated Parmesan cheese

- 2 Small, long soft rolls, such as hero, hoagie, or Italian sub rolls (gluten-free, if a concern), split open lengthwise

Directions:

1. Preheat the air fryer to 350°F .

2. When the machine is at temperature, coat both sides of the eggplant slices with olive oil spray. Set them in the basket in one layer and air-fry undisturbed for 10 minutes, until lightly browned and softened.

3. Increase the machine's temperature to 375°F (or 370°F, if that's the closest setting—unless the machine is already at 360°F, in which case leave it alone). Top each eggplant slice with 2 teaspoons pizza sauce, then 1 tablespoon cheese. Air-fry undisturbed for 2 minutes, or until the cheese has melted.

4. Use a nonstick-safe spatula, and perhaps a flatware fork for balance, to transfer the eggplant slices cheese side up to a cutting board. Set the roll(s) cut side down in the basket in one layer (working in batches as necessary) and air-fry undisturbed for 1 minute, to toast the rolls a bit and warm them up. Set 2 eggplant slices in each warm roll.

Chicken Saltimbocca Sandwiches

Servings: 3

Cooking Time: 11 Minutes

Ingredients:

- 3 5- to 6-ounce boneless skinless chicken breasts
- 6 Thin prosciutto slices
- 6 Provolone cheese slices
- 3 Long soft rolls, such as hero, hoagie, or Italian sub rolls (gluten-free, if a concern), split open lengthwise

- 3 tablespoons Pesto, purchased or homemade (see the headnote)

Directions:

1. Preheat the air fryer to 400°F.

2. Wrap each chicken breast with 2 prosciutto slices, spiraling the prosciutto around the breast and overlapping the slices a bit to cover the breast. The prosciutto will stick to the chicken more readily than bacon does.

3. When the machine is at temperature, set the wrapped chicken breasts in the basket and air-fry undisturbed for 10 minutes, or until the prosciutto is frizzled and the chicken is cooked through.

4. Overlap 2 cheese slices on each breast. Air-fry undisturbed for 1 minute, or until melted. Take the basket out of the machine.

5. Smear the insides of the rolls with the pesto, then use kitchen tongs to put a wrapped and cheesy chicken breast in each roll.

Sausage And Pepper Heros

Servings: 3

Cooking Time: 11 Minutes

Ingredients:

- 3 links (about 9 ounces total) Sweet Italian sausages (gluten-free, if a concern)
- 1½ Medium red or green bell pepper(s), stemmed, cored, and cut into ½-inch-wide strips
- 1 medium Yellow or white onion(s), peeled, halved, and sliced into thin half-moons
- 3 Long soft rolls, such as hero, hoagie, or Italian sub rolls (gluten-free, if a concern), split open lengthwise
- For garnishing Balsamic vinegar
- For garnishing Fresh basil leaves

Directions:

1. Preheat the air fryer to 400°F.

2. When the machine is at temperature, set the sausage links in the basket in one layer and air-fry undisturbed for 5 minutes.

3. Add the pepper strips and onions. Continue air-frying, tossing and rearranging everything about once every minute, for 5 minutes, or until the sausages are browned and an instant-read meat thermometer inserted into one of the links registers 160°F.

4. Use a nonstick-safe spatula and kitchen tongs to transfer the sausages and vegetables to a cutting board. Set the rolls cut side down in the basket in one layer (working in batches as necessary) and air-fry undisturbed for 1 minute, to toast the rolls a bit and warm them up. Set 1 sausage with some pepper strips and onions in each warm roll, sprinkle balsamic vinegar over the sandwich fillings, and garnish with basil leaves.

Perfect Burgers

Servings: 3
Cooking Time: 13 Minutes

Ingredients:

- 1 pound 2 ounces 90% lean ground beef
- 1½ tablespoons Worcestershire sauce (gluten-free, if a concern)
- ½ teaspoon Ground black pepper
- 3 Hamburger buns (gluten-free if a concern), split open

Directions:

1. Preheat the air fryer to 375°F .

2. Gently mix the ground beef, Worcestershire sauce, and pepper in a bowl until well combined but preserving as much of the meat's fibers as possible. Divide this mixture into two 5-inch patties for the small batch, three 5-inch patties for the medium, or four 5-inch patties for the large. Make a thumbprint indentation in the center of each patty, about halfway through the meat.

3. Set the patties in the basket in one layer with some space between them. Air-fry undisturbed for 10 minutes, or until an instant-read meat thermometer inserted into the center of a burger registers 160°F (a medium-well burger). You may need to add 2 minutes cooking time if the air fryer is at 360°F.

4. Use a nonstick-safe spatula, and perhaps a flatware fork for balance, to transfer the burgers to a cutting board. Set the buns cut side down in the basket in one layer (working in batches as necessary) and air-fry undisturbed for 1 minute, to toast a bit and warm up. Serve the burgers in the warm buns.

Asian Glazed Meatballs

Servings: 4
Cooking Time: 10 Minutes

Ingredients:

- 1 large shallot, finely chopped
- 2 cloves garlic, minced
- 1 tablespoon grated fresh ginger
- 2 teaspoons fresh thyme, finely chopped
- 1½ cups brown mushrooms, very finely chopped (a food processor works well here)
- 2 tablespoons soy sauce
- freshly ground black pepper
- 1 pound ground beef
- ½ pound ground pork
- 3 egg yolks
- 1 cup Thai sweet chili sauce (spring roll sauce)
- ¼ cup toasted sesame seeds
- 2 scallions, sliced

Directions:

1. Combine the shallot, garlic, ginger, thyme, mushrooms, soy sauce, freshly ground black pepper, ground beef and pork, and egg yolks in a bowl and mix the ingredients together. Gently shape the mixture into 24 balls, about the size of a golf ball.

2. Preheat the air fryer to 380°F.

3. Working in batches, air-fry the meatballs for 8 minutes, turning the meatballs over halfway through the cooking time. Drizzle some of the Thai sweet chili sauce on top of each meatball and return the basket to the air fryer, air-frying for another 2 minutes. Reserve the remaining Thai sweet chili sauce for serving.

4. As soon as the meatballs are done, sprinkle with toasted sesame seeds and transfer them to a serving platter. Scatter the scallions around and serve warm.

Fish And Seafood Recipes

Five Spice Red Snapper With Green Onions And Orange Salsa

Servings: 2
Cooking Time: 8 Minutes

Ingredients:

- 2 oranges, peeled, segmented and chopped
- 1 tablespoon minced shallot
- 1 to 3 teaspoons minced red Jalapeño or Serrano pepper
- 1 tablespoon chopped fresh cilantro
- lime juice, to taste
- salt, to taste
- 2 (5- to 6-ounce) red snapper fillets
- ½ teaspoon Chinese five spice powder
- salt and freshly ground black pepper
- vegetable or olive oil, in a spray bottle
- 4 green onions, cut into 2-inch lengths

Directions:

1. Start by making the salsa. Cut the peel off the oranges, slicing around the oranges to expose the flesh. Segment the oranges by cutting in between the membranes of the orange. Chop the segments roughly and combine in a bowl with the shallot, Jalapeño or Serrano pepper, cilantro, lime juice and salt. Set the salsa aside.
2. Preheat the air fryer to 400°F.
3. Season the fish fillets with the five-spice powder, salt and freshly ground black pepper. Spray both sides of the fish fillets with oil. Toss the green onions with a little oil.
4. Transfer the fish to the air fryer basket and scatter the green onions around the fish. Air-fry at 400°F for 8 minutes.

5. Remove the fish from the air fryer, along with the fried green onions. Serve with white rice and a spoonful of the salsa on top.

Lightened-up Breaded Fish Filets

Servings: 4
Cooking Time: 10 Minutes

Ingredients:

- ½ cup all-purpose flour
- ½ teaspoon cayenne pepper
- 1 teaspoon garlic powder
- ½ teaspoon black pepper
- ¼ teaspoon salt
- 2 eggs, whisked
- 1½ cups panko breadcrumbs
- 1 pound boneless white fish filets
- 1 cup tartar sauce
- 1 lemon, sliced into wedges

Directions:

1. In a medium bowl, mix the flour, cayenne pepper, garlic powder, pepper, and salt.
2. In a shallow dish, place the eggs.
3. In a third dish, place the breadcrumbs.
4. Cover the fish in the flour, dip them in the egg, and coat them with panko. Repeat until all fish are covered in the breading.
5. Liberally spray the metal trivet that fits inside the air fryer basket with olive oil mist. Place the fish onto the trivet, leaving space between the filets to flip. Cook for 5 minutes, flip the fish, and cook another 5 minutes. Repeat until all the fish is cooked.
6. Serve warm with tartar sauce and lemon wedges.

Fried Shrimp

Servings:3
Cooking Time: 7 Minutes

Ingredients:
- 1 Large egg white
- 2 tablespoons Water
- 1 cup Plain dried bread crumbs (gluten-free, if a concern)
- ¼ cup All-purpose flour or almond flour
- ¼ cup Yellow cornmeal
- 1 teaspoon Celery salt
- 1 teaspoon Mild paprika
- Up to ½ teaspoon Cayenne (optional)
- ¾ pound Large shrimp (20–25 per pound), peeled and deveined
- Vegetable oil spray

Directions:
1. Preheat the air fryer to 400°F.
2. Set two medium or large bowls on your counter. In the first, whisk the egg white and water until foamy. In the second, stir the bread crumbs, flour, cornmeal, celery salt, paprika, and cayenne (if using) until well combined.
3. Pour all the shrimp into the egg white mixture and stir gently until all the shrimp are coated. Use kitchen tongs to pick them up one by one and transfer them to the bread-crumb mixture. Turn each in the bread-crumb mixture to coat it evenly and thoroughly on all sides before setting it on a cutting board. When you're done coating the shrimp, coat them all on both sides with the vegetable oil spray.
4. Set the shrimp in as close to one layer in the basket as you can. Some may overlap. Air-fry for 7 minutes, gently rearranging the shrimp at the 4-minute mark to get covered surfaces exposed, until golden brown and firm but not hard.
5. Use kitchen tongs to gently transfer the shrimp to a wire rack. Cool for only a minute or two before serving.

Salmon Puttanesca En Papillotte With Zucchini

Servings: 2
Cooking Time: 17 Minutes

Ingredients:
- 1 small zucchini, sliced into ¼-inch thick half moons
- 1 teaspoon olive oil
- salt and freshly ground black pepper
- 2 (5-ounce) salmon fillets
- 1 beefsteak tomato, chopped (about 1 cup)
- 1 tablespoon capers, rinsed
- 10 black olives, pitted and sliced
- 2 tablespoons dry vermouth or white wine 2 tablespoons butter
- ¼ cup chopped fresh basil, chopped

Directions:
1. Preheat the air fryer to 400°F.
2. Toss the zucchini with the olive oil, salt and freshly ground black pepper. Transfer the zucchini into the air fryer basket and air-fry for 5 minutes, shaking the basket once or twice during the cooking process.
3. Cut out 2 large rectangles of parchment paper – about 13-inches by 15-inches each. Divide the air-fried zucchini between the two pieces of parchment paper, placing the vegetables in the center of each rectangle.
4. Place a fillet of salmon on each pile of zucchini. Season the fish very well with salt and pepper. Toss the tomato, capers, olives and vermouth (or white wine) together in a bowl. Divide the tomato mixture between the two fish

packages, placing it on top of the fish fillets and pouring any juice out of the bowl onto the fish. Top each fillet with a tablespoon of butter.

5. Fold up each parchment square. Bring two edges together and fold them over a few times, leaving some space above the fish. Twist the open sides together and upwards so they can serve as handles for the packet, but don't let them extend beyond the top of the air fryer basket.

6. Place the two packages into the air fryer and air-fry at 400°F for 12 minutes. The packages should be puffed up and slightly browned when fully cooked. Once cooked, let the fish sit in the parchment for 2 minutes.

7. Serve the fish in the parchment paper, or if desired, remove the parchment paper before serving. Garnish with a little fresh basil.

Beer-breaded Halibut Fish Tacos

Servings: 4
Cooking Time: 10 Minutes

Ingredients:
- 1 pound halibut, cut into 1-inch strips
- 1 cup light beer
- 1 jalapeño, minced and divided
- 1 clove garlic, minced
- ¼ teaspoon ground cumin
- ½ cup cornmeal
- ¼ cup all-purpose flour
- 1¼ teaspoons sea salt, divided
- 2 cups shredded cabbage
- 1 lime, juiced and divided
- ¼ cup Greek yogurt
- ¼ cup mayonnaise
- 1 cup grape tomatoes, quartered
- ½ cup chopped cilantro
- ¼ cup chopped onion
- 1 egg, whisked
- 8 corn tortillas

Directions:
1. In a shallow baking dish, place the fish, the beer, 1 teaspoon of the minced jalapeño, the garlic, and the cumin. Cover and refrigerate for 30 minutes.

2. Meanwhile, in a medium bowl, mix together the cornmeal, flour, and ½ teaspoon of the salt.

3. In large bowl, mix together the shredded cabbage, 1 tablespoon of the lime juice, the Greek yogurt, the mayonnaise, and ½ teaspoon of the salt.

4. In a small bowl, make the pico de gallo by mixing together the tomatoes, cilantro, onion, ¼ teaspoon of the salt, the remaining jalapeño, and the remaining lime juice.

5. Remove the fish from the refrigerator and discard the marinade. Dredge the fish in the whisked egg; then dredge the fish in the cornmeal flour mixture, until all pieces of fish have been breaded.

6. Preheat the air fryer to 350°F.

7. Place the fish in the air fryer basket and spray liberally with cooking spray. Cook for 6 minutes, flip and shake the fish, and cook another 4 minutes.

8. While the fish is cooking, heat the tortillas in a heavy skillet for 1 to 2 minutes over high heat.

9. To assemble the tacos, place the battered fish on the heated tortillas, and top with slaw and pico de gallo. Serve immediately.

Horseradish-crusted Salmon Fillets

Servings:3

Cooking Time: 8 Minutes

Ingredients:

- ½ cup Fresh bread crumbs (see the headnote)
- 4 tablespoons (¼ cup/½ stick) Butter, melted and cooled
- ¼ cup Jarred prepared white horseradish
- Vegetable oil spray
- 4 6-ounce skin-on salmon fillets (for more information, see here)

Directions:

1. Preheat the air fryer to 400°F.
2. Mix the bread crumbs, butter, and horseradish in a bowl until well combined.
3. Take the basket out of the machine. Generously spray the skin side of each fillet. Pick them up one by one with a nonstick-safe spatula and set them in the basket skin side down with as much air space between them as possible. Divide the bread-crumb mixture between the fillets, coating the top of each fillet with an even layer. Generously coat the bread-crumb mixture with vegetable oil spray.
4. Return the basket to the machine and air-fry undisturbed for 8 minutes, or until the topping has lightly browned and the fish is firm but not hard.
5. Use a nonstick-safe spatula to transfer the salmon fillets to serving plates. Cool for 5 minutes before serving. Because of the butter in the topping, it will stay very hot for quite a while. Take care, especially if you're serving these fillets to children.

Popcorn Crawfish

Servings: 4

Cooking Time: 18 Minutes

Ingredients:

- ½ cup flour, plus 2 tablespoons
- ½ teaspoon garlic powder
- 1½ teaspoons Old Bay Seasoning
- ½ teaspoon onion powder
- ½ cup beer, plus 2 tablespoons
- 12-ounce package frozen crawfish tail meat, thawed and drained
- oil for misting or cooking spray
- Coating
- 1½ cups panko crumbs
- 1 teaspoon Old Bay Seasoning
- ½ teaspoon ground black pepper

Directions:

1. In a large bowl, mix together the flour, garlic powder, Old Bay Seasoning, and onion powder. Stir in beer to blend.
2. Add crawfish meat to batter and stir to coat.
3. Combine the coating ingredients in food processor and pulse to finely crush the crumbs. Transfer crumbs to shallow dish.
4. Preheat air fryer to 390°F.
5. Pour the crawfish and batter into a colander to drain. Stir with a spoon to drain excess batter.
6. Working with a handful of crawfish at a time, roll in crumbs and place on a cookie sheet. It's okay if some of the smaller pieces of crawfish meat stick together.
7. Spray breaded crawfish with oil or cooking spray and place all at once into air fryer basket.
8. Cook at 390°F for 5minutes. Shake basket or stir and mist again with olive oil or spray. Cook 5 moreminutes, shake basket again, and mist lightly again. Continue cooking 5 more minutes, until browned and crispy.

Lobster Tails With Lemon Garlic Butter

Servings: 2

Cooking Time: 5 Minutes

Ingredients:

- 4 ounces unsalted butter
- 1 tablespoon finely chopped lemon zest
- 1 clove garlic, thinly sliced
- 2 (6-ounce) lobster tails
- salt and freshly ground black pepper
- ½ cup white wine
- ½ lemon, sliced
- vegetable oil

Directions:

1. Start by making the lemon garlic butter. Combine the butter, lemon zest and garlic in a small saucepan. Melt and simmer the butter on the stovetop over the lowest possible heat while you prepare the lobster tails.

2. Prepare the lobster tails by cutting down the middle of the top of the shell. Crack the bottom shell by squeezing the sides of the lobster together so that you can access the lobster meat inside. Pull the lobster tail up out of the shell, but leave it attached at the base of the tail. Lay the lobster meat on top of the shell and season with salt and freshly ground black pepper. Pour a little of the lemon garlic butter on top of the lobster meat and transfer the lobster to the refrigerator so that the butter solidifies a little.

3. Pour the white wine into the air fryer drawer and add the lemon slices. Preheat the air fryer to 400°F for 5 minutes.

4. Transfer the lobster tails to the air fryer basket. Air-fry at 370° for 5 minutes, brushing more butter on halfway through cooking. (Add a minute or two if your lobster tail is more than 6-ounces.) Remove and serve with more butter for dipping or drizzling.

Horseradish Crusted Salmon

Servings: 2

Cooking Time: 14 Minutes

Ingredients:

- 2 (5-ounce) salmon fillets
- salt and freshly ground black pepper
- 2 teaspoons Dijon mustard
- ½ cup panko breadcrumbs*
- 2 tablespoons prepared horseradish
- ½ teaspoon finely chopped lemon zest
- 1 tablespoon olive oil
- 1 tablespoon chopped fresh parsley

Directions:

1. Preheat the air fryer to 360°F.

2. Season the salmon with salt and freshly ground black pepper. Then spread the Dijon mustard on the salmon, coating the entire surface.

3. Combine the breadcrumbs, horseradish, lemon zest and olive oil in a small bowl. Spread the mixture over the top of the salmon and press down lightly with your hands, adhering it to the salmon using the mustard as "glue".

4. Transfer the salmon to the air fryer basket and air-fry at 360°F for 14 minutes (depending on how thick your fillet is) or until the fish feels firm to the touch. Sprinkle with the parsley.

Nutty Shrimp With Amaretto Glaze

Servings: 10

Cooking Time: 10 Minutes

Ingredients:

- 1 cup flour
- ½ teaspoon baking powder
- 1 teaspoon salt
- 2 eggs, beaten
- ½ cup milk
- 2 tablespoons olive or vegetable oil
- 2 cups sliced almonds
- 2 pounds large shrimp (about 32 to 40 shrimp), peeled and deveined, tails left on
- 2 cups amaretto liqueur

Directions:

1. Combine the flour, baking powder and salt in a large bowl. Add the eggs, milk and oil and stir until it forms a smooth batter. Coarsely crush the sliced almonds into a second shallow dish with your hands.

2. Dry the shrimp well with paper towels. Dip the shrimp into the batter and shake off any excess batter, leaving just enough to lightly coat the shrimp. Transfer the shrimp to the dish with the almonds and coat completely. Place the coated shrimp on a plate or baking sheet and when all the shrimp have been coated, freeze the shrimp for an 1 hour, or as long as a week before air-frying.

3. Preheat the air fryer to 400°F.

4. Transfer 8 frozen shrimp at a time to the air fryer basket. Air-fry for 6 minutes. Turn the shrimp over and air-fry for an additional 4 minutes. Repeat with the remaining shrimp.

5. While the shrimp are cooking, bring the Amaretto to a boil in a small saucepan on the stovetop. Lower the heat and simmer until it has reduced and thickened into a glaze – about 10 minutes.

6. Remove the shrimp from the air fryer and brush both sides with the warm amaretto glaze. Serve warm.

Sea Scallops

Servings: 4

Cooking Time: 8 Minutes

Ingredients:

- 1½ pounds sea scallops
- salt and pepper
- 2 eggs
- ½ cup flour
- ½ cup plain breadcrumbs
- oil for misting or cooking spray

Directions:

1. Rinse scallops and remove the tough side muscle. Sprinkle to taste with salt and pepper.

2. Beat eggs together in a shallow dish. Place flour in a second shallow dish and breadcrumbs in a third.

3. Preheat air fryer to 390°F.

4. Dip scallops in flour, then eggs, and then roll in breadcrumbs. Mist with oil or cooking spray.

5. Place scallops in air fryer basket in a single layer, leaving some space between. You should be able to cook about a dozen at a time.

6. Cook at 390°F for 8 minutes, watching carefully so as not to overcook. Scallops are done when they turn opaque all the way through. They will feel slightly firm when pressed with tines of a fork.

7. Repeat step 6 to cook remaining scallops.

Miso-rubbed Salmon Fillets

Servings:3

Cooking Time: 5 Minutes

Ingredients:

- ¼ cup White (shiro) miso paste (usually made from rice and soy beans)
- 1½ tablespoons Mirin or a substitute (see here)
- 2½ teaspoons Unseasoned rice vinegar (see here)
- Vegetable oil spray
- 3 6-ounce skin-on salmon fillets (for more information, see here)

Directions:

1. Preheat the air fryer to 400°F.
2. Mix the miso, mirin, and vinegar in a small bowl until uniform.
3. Remove the basket from the machine. Generously spray the skin side of each fillet. Pick them up one by one with a nonstick-safe spatula and set them in the basket skin side down with as much air space between them as possible. Coat the top of each fillet with the miso mixture, dividing it evenly between them.
4. Return the basket to the machine. Air-fry undisturbed for 5 minutes, or until lightly browned and firm.
5. Use a nonstick-safe spatula to transfer the fillets to serving plates. Cool for only a minute or so before serving.

Curried Sweet-and-spicy Scallops

Servings:3
Cooking Time: 5 Minutes

Ingredients:

- 6 tablespoons Thai sweet chili sauce
- 2 cups (from about 5 cups cereal) Crushed Rice Krispies or other rice-puff cereal
- 2 teaspoons Yellow curry powder, purchased or homemade (see here)
- 1 pound Sea scallops
- Vegetable oil spray

Directions:

1. Preheat the air fryer to 400°F.
2. Set up and fill two shallow soup plates or small pie plates on your counter: one for the chili sauce and one for crumbs, mixed with the curry powder.
3. Dip a scallop into the chili sauce, coating it on all sides. Set it in the cereal mixture and turn several times to coat evenly. Gently shake off any excess and set the scallop on a cutting board. Continue dipping and coating the remaining scallops. Coat them all on all sides with the vegetable oil spray.
4. Set the scallops in the basket with as much air space between them as possible. Air-fry undisturbed for 5 minutes, or until lightly browned and crunchy.
5. Remove the basket. Set aside for 2 minutes to let the coating set up. Then gently pour the contents of the basket onto a platter and serve at once.

Fried Scallops

Servings:3
Cooking Time: 6 Minutes

Ingredients:
- ½ cup All-purpose flour or tapioca flour
- 1 Large egg(s), well beaten
- 2 cups Corn flake crumbs (gluten-free, if a concern)
- Up to 2 teaspoons Cayenne
- 1 teaspoon Celery seeds
- 1 teaspoon Table salt
- 1 pound Sea scallops
- Vegetable oil spray

Directions:
1. Preheat the air fryer to 400°F.
2. Set up and fill three shallow soup plates or small pie plates on your counter: one for the flour; one for the beaten egg(s); and one for the corn flake crumbs, stirred with the cayenne, celery seeds, and salt until well combined.
3. One by one, dip a scallop in the flour, turning it every way to coat it thoroughly. Gently shake off any excess flour, then dip the scallop in the egg(s), turning it again to coat all sides. Let any excess egg slip back into the rest, then set the scallop in the corn flake mixture. Turn it several times, pressing gently to get an even coating on the scallop all around. Generously coat the scallop with vegetable oil spray, then set it aside on a cutting board. Coat the remaining scallops in the same way.
4. Set the scallops in the basket with as much air space between them as possible. They should not touch. Air-fry undisturbed for 6 minutes, or until lightly browned and firm.

5. Use kitchen tongs to gently transfer the scallops to a wire rack. Cool for only a minute or two before serving.

Fish And "chips"

Servings: 2
Cooking Time: 10 Minutes

Ingredients:
- ½ cup flour
- ½ teaspoon paprika
- ¼ teaspoon ground white pepper (or freshly ground black pepper)
- 1 egg
- ¼ cup mayonnaise
- 2 cups salt & vinegar kettle cooked potato chips, coarsely crushed
- 12 ounces cod
- tartar sauce
- lemon wedges

Directions:
1. Set up a dredging station. Combine the flour, paprika and pepper in a shallow dish. Combine the egg and mayonnaise in a second shallow dish. Place the crushed potato chips in a third shallow dish.
2. Cut the cod into 6 pieces. Dredge each piece of fish in the flour, then dip it into the egg mixture and then place it into the crushed potato chips. Make sure all sides of the fish are covered and pat the chips gently onto the fish so they stick well.
3. Preheat the air fryer to 370°F.
4. Place the coated fish fillets into the air fry basket. (It is ok if a couple of pieces slightly overlap or rest on top of other fillets in order to fit everything in the basket.)

5. Air-fry for 10 minutes, gently turning the fish over halfway through the cooking time.

6. Transfer the fish to a platter and serve with tartar sauce and lemon wedges.

Tilapia Teriyaki

Servings: 3

Cooking Time: 10 Minutes

Ingredients:

- 4 tablespoons teriyaki sauce
- 1 tablespoon pineapple juice
- 1 pound tilapia fillets
- cooking spray
- 6 ounces frozen mixed peppers with onions, thawed and drained
- 2 cups cooked rice

Directions:

1. Mix the teriyaki sauce and pineapple juice together in a small bowl.

2. Split tilapia fillets down the center lengthwise.

3. Brush all sides of fish with the sauce, spray air fryer basket with nonstick cooking spray, and place fish in the basket.

4. Stir the peppers and onions into the remaining sauce and spoon over the fish. Save any leftover sauce for drizzling over the fish when serving.

5. Cook at 360°F for 10 minutes, until fish flakes easily with a fork and is done in center.

6. Divide into 3 or 4 servings and serve each with approximately ½ cup cooked rice.

Stuffed Shrimp

Servings: 4

Cooking Time: 12 Minutes Per Batch

Ingredients:

- 16 tail-on shrimp, peeled and deveined (last tail section intact)
- ¾ cup crushed panko breadcrumbs
- oil for misting or cooking spray
- Stuffing
- 2 6-ounce cans lump crabmeat
- 2 tablespoons chopped shallots
- 2 tablespoons chopped green onions
- 2 tablespoons chopped celery
- 2 tablespoons chopped green bell pepper
- ½ cup crushed saltine crackers
- 1 teaspoon Old Bay Seasoning
- 1 teaspoon garlic powder
- ¼ teaspoon ground thyme
- 2 teaspoons dried parsley flakes
- 2 teaspoons fresh lemon juice
- 2 teaspoons Worcestershire sauce
- 1 egg, beaten

Directions:

1. Rinse shrimp. Remove tail section (shell) from 4 shrimp, discard, and chop the meat finely.

2. To prepare the remaining 12 shrimp, cut a deep slit down the back side so that the meat lies open flat. Do not cut all the way through.

3. Preheat air fryer to 360°F.

4. Place chopped shrimp in a large bowl with all of the stuffing ingredients and stir to combine.

5. Divide stuffing into 12 portions, about 2 tablespoons each.

6. Place one stuffing portion onto the back of each shrimp and form into a ball or oblong shape. Press firmly so that stuffing sticks together and adheres to shrimp.

7. Gently roll each stuffed shrimp in panko crumbs and mist with oil or cooking spray.

8. Place 6 shrimp in air fryer basket and cook at 360°F for 10minutes. Mist with oil or spray and cook 2 minutes longer or until stuffing cooks through inside and is crispy outside.

9. Repeat step 8 to cook remaining shrimp.

Printed by Libri Plureos GmbH in Hamburg,
Germany